GOOD NEWS STUDIES

Consulting Editor: Robert J. Karris, O.F.M.

Volume 10

Experiencing the Good News

The New Testament as Communication

by

James M. Reese, O.S.F.S.

Michael Glazier, Inc.

Wilmington, Delaware

About the Author
James M. Reese, O.S.F.S., is Associate Professor of Theology at St. John's University in New York City. He is a member of the editorial staff of *The Bible Today* and *Biblical Theology Bulletin*, and has worked with continuing education programs for clergy and religious. His most recent books are *Jesus, His Word and Work*, a study-guide to the Synoptic Gospels; *1 and 2 Thessalonians*, Volume 16 of the *New Testament Message* series; and *The Book of Wisdom, Song of Songs*, Volume 20 of the *Old Testament Message* series.

First published in 1984 by Michael Glazier, Inc., 1723 Delaware Avenue, Wilmington, DE 19806.

Library of Congress Cataloging in Publication Data
Reese, James M.
   The New Testament As Communication
   (Good news studies; v. 10)
   Includes bibliographies.
   1. Bible. N.T.—Criticism, interpretation, etc.
   2. Bible. N.T.—Hermeneutics.
   3. Revelation.
   4. Communication (Theology)
I. Title.
II. Series.
BS2361.2.R44   1984   225.6'01   84-81403
ISBN 0-89453-448-3

International Standard Book Number Good News Studies: 0-89453-290-1

Typography by Richard Huber
Printed in the United States of America

CONTENTS

Indexes

Introduction

For many years biblical commentators have been calling for the incorporation of what the French call "the human sciences" into New Testament interpretation. This book responds to that call. A global statement of what is at stake is found in the article on the need by Pierre Grelot in the June 1976 issue of *Nouvelle Revue Théologique*. Actually, much of the groundwork for this effort is available in the writings of Eugene A. Nida, many of which were composed in connection with his preparation of transcultural aids for translators of the Bible.

I have been concerned with this problem in teaching a course on Interpreting the Bible for theology majors. A research leave from St. John's University in New York City gave me the opportunity to prepare a synthetic presentation of the question. I raised some of these questions in my book *Preaching God's Burning Word* (Liturgical Press, 1975). In Part I, I review recent work in literary criticism and semiotics related to the language revolution as they apply to the New Testament. To this review I join insights on religious imagination and language in Part II. The finished product is primarily descriptive of developments by anthropologists-linguists, social critics and theologians of culture.

My primary goal is to encourage concerned students to recognize that there are many ways of reading the inspired writings of the early Christian Church. I quote briefly from a variety of modern authors to give a taste of contemporary style as well as an overview of content. Further material is available in the "sources" cited at the end of each chapter.

For this project to be successful, the cooperation of readers is crucial. They must view this as an introduction and undertake the task of becoming in some sense "authors" of what they read. As Amos Wilder put it poetically, "But there is such a thing as a feel for reality which only needs to be instructed. Sometimes our laymen (like babes) can alert their instructors!" (from a letter to me on December 6, 1983).

My thanks to the administration of St. John's University, and especially to those who expedited my research leave: Vice President and Dean, the Reverend Thomas F. Hoar, C.M., Dean Paul Medici and Chair Person of the Department of Theology, the Reverend John H. McKenna, C.M. I thank my confreres in the Oblates of St. Francis de Sales at the DeSales Theological Center in Washington, D.C., for their warm welcome, generous hospitality and joyful spirit of celebration during my year of research.

In a special way I offer this work in gratitude to Eugene A. Nida and Amos N. Wilder, whose long years of enthusiastic seminal scholarship provide the basis for this approach — as my many references to their work reveal. Their encouragement shaped my efforts to provide a new generation of students with help in undertaking the task of developing their personal method of interpreting the New Testament.

JMR
Feast of SS Philip and James

Part I

Language as a System of Communication

Chapter 1

The Elements of Language

Language is the principal means of human communication. The first part of this book illustrates implications of the modern language explosion for developing a linguistic method of interpreting the New Testament, the normative religious library for the Christian community. This chapter will propose a descriptive definition of language. Then it will elaborate on that definition as the first step toward explaining how language functions in interpreting these basic Christian texts.

My proposed definition: a language is a complete, self-regulating system of verbal symbols encoded by verbal gesture to be decoded by human ears for sharing experience and communicating meaning in a given cultural context. This definition embraces four essential qualities about language that will be explained in Points A to D.

Point A. Every language is a potentially comprehensive system, that is, it covers the entire area of communication necessary for the group that uses it.

Point B. Every language is a stratified sign system of sounds, syntax and meaning. Its signs are conventional objects, that is, perceptible forms that convey meaning.

These forms are primarily audible, but in most languages they have been visualized in pictures or letters so that the language can be preserved in writing. At present there seem to be about 5,000 natural languages or sound-meaning systems in the world. In fact, one ethnologist has listed 5103 languages (Kopesec: 2). This figure is disputed; some estimates are as low as 2,500. The number depends to some extent on whether to call certain variations languages or simply dialects.

The signs of a language belong simultaneously to three strata or networks: 1) syntax or the grammatical network; 2) semantics or the meaning network; 3) pragmatics or the informational network.

1) The grammatical network deals with the relationship of meaningful sounds among themselves. I say "meaningful" sounds because many sounds have no meaning in individual languages. Hence, in each language simple sounds or "ultimate phonic elements" are formed into meaningful sounds called phonemes, that is, sounds capable of differentiating words within a given language. Phonemes combine to make up the vocabulary or lexicon of that language (Jakobson: 23-27). For example, Americans can easily recognize that a Polish sentence is not English. Why? Because the words have combinations of letters that are impossible in English. Technically, then, Polish uses different phonemes or basic sounds than English.

Syntax is the formal system by which a language operates as a set of rules determining what sound relationships are permissible. Syntax thus includes both phonemics and grammar. Phonemics governs how individual speech sounds are formed into patterns acceptable in the language. Grammar is the pattern of relationships permitted between all types of verbal units: words, phrases, clauses, sentences, paragraphs.

Over and above these formational rules for surface syntax, the syntax network includes transformational grammar, that is, the study of how a language generates its syntax.

Example. Rom 9:5. The translation of this verse is disputed

because its syntax is unclear. A comparison of English translations shows that some editors divide the verse into two sentences and make God the subject of the second. Other editors see only one sentence with Christ as subject. Hence, the impact of syntax on meaning.

2) Semantics treats the relation of verbal signs to concepts and objects, that is, the rules governing the conditions under which signs express meaning. The next chapter will elaborate on the universal or deep semantic components of language.

Example. Eph 1:3-10. In the Greek text this complex blessing consists of a single complicated sentence. It is difficult to determine antecedents of pronouns and so to fix the role of the Father and of Jesus in the working out of salvation. Translators have to break down the semantic content into shorter sentences in order to communicate the meaning in English.

3) Pragmatics is the "relation of elements and their sequences to extra-linguistic information" (Oller: 50). Pragmatic rules differ greatly from language to language. Pragmatics refers to how a language packages it information. It treats the way words, phrases and sentences relate the subject matter to the knowledge of readers. Thus, some languages cannot use rhetorical questions; others do not have articles; others must use polite forms in addressing certain persons. Such pragmatic rules depend to a great extent on cultural factors. Within any given language they tend to be less stable than the rules of syntax and semantics because they impinge upon the rhetorical, psychological and cultural dimensions of communication events or speech acts. The same semantic content can be structured in a wide variety of ways in different languages. Pragmatics reveals language as a system of behavior that creates a "universe of discourse" for speakers and hearers who constantly interact with both linguistic and nonlinguistic contexts. In this sense, "The language of a people is its fate" (Wilder: Chapter 1).

These three networks of signs do not operate in the same

way. That is the principal reason why languages are difficult to master, constantly changing, often ambiguous, but also powerful means of communication. Hearers and readers can diagram surface syntactic relations, but they cannot see directly the underlying semantic blocks that form part of a verbal sign or lexeme. Lexeme, the technical term, is more accurate for verbal sign than "word," because the same lexeme appears in a variety of forms, like: see, saw, seen; man, men. The semantic components must be isolated by logical analysis of the surface structure into meaning kernels (see Chapter 2). The pragmatic network embraces that potential openness that demands speaker or hearer participation in understanding the speech event (see Chapter 7).

Example. 2 Cor 7:9. Paul refers to the semantic effect that his earlier letter had in changing the conduct of his hearers by drawing them to repent.

In written communication certain elements of the vocal gesture are lost or decreased, such as pitch, stress, duration, dramatic pause, irony, tone of voice and other emotional nuances. These can be recovered to some extent by figures of speech and of language, or by explicit commentary, but the oral nature of human language is the primary form of human communication (see Chapters 7 and 8).

Example. Rom 8:31-39. By means of a series of rhetorical questions and then shifting into the inclusive first person, Paul captures the dialogic nature of the salvation communicated by the Father in Christ through the Holy Spirit.

Point C. Every language is a symbolic system, that is, it is made up of arbitrary or conventional sound signs. In other words, in language the relation between the form of individual signs and their meanings is determined by the language group. Charles S. Peirce's research on signs provided a basis for the science of semiotics, which offers fruitful insights into understanding how language communicates meaning. For Peirce, all thinking is interpretation with signs and functions by forming a continuity with previous thinking. Language acts as a vehicle for communicating all dimensions of meaning because it symbolizes the threefold process that is characteristic of all relationships: 1) immediacy — or the presence of objects to themselves (which he calls first-ness); 2) opposition — or contrasting objects with one another (which he calls secondness); 3) mediation — or relating objects to each other (which he calls thirdness).

By symbolizing the acts of perceiving, judging and discerning, language empowers humans to relate to persons, to objects and to processes and thus to experience reality, to know or reject truth, to choose good or evil, to communicate with or deceive one another (Fitzgerald). Peirce was neither a systematic nor consistent thinker, nor are his collected papers easy to understand. Yet his influence has been powerful on the modern language explosion and it will be incorporated into this study, often through the research of Eugene A. Nida.

Language symbols are signs because they point beyond themselves to concepts and ultimately designate objects. They must be distinguished from two other forms of signs: indexes and icons. An index is a sign that in some way touches what it points toward, like smoke toward a fire, or a weather vane toward the flow of wind. An icon in some way resembles the object it stands for, as a photograph reveals the contours of the human face, or a diagram maps out relationships within a system.

Point D. Charles Peirce defined a sign as "anything which determines something else (its *interpretant*) to refer to an object to which itself refers (its object) in the same way, the interpretant becoming in turn a sign and so on *ad infinitum*" (*Collected Papers* 2:169). The key to his definition is the interpretant, which is "the translatability of every verbal sign into another, more explicit one" (Jakobson: 77). A language has the capacity to explain and clarify its own symbols and thus identify its constituent elements. Language interpretants are paraphrases in which one paradigmatic element takes the place of another. In this way language plays a mediating role in human communication. It provides a meaningful context for every symbol within its given syntactic structures (Nida: 199).

Application to New Testament Interpretation. How does all of this technical information about language relate to an understanding of the New Testament? Ultimately because language is the mode of communication uniquely human. Language symbols are natural expressions of human values. They stimulate senders (encoders) and influence recipients (decoders) and provide both with a personal means of mutual communication. Parts of the New Testament have been translated into over 1,500 of the estimated 5,000 languages now in use throughout the world. Each of these languages has its own set of phonemes that make up its system of meaningful sounds. As stated above, these sounds combine to form the language's lexicon or vocabulary. A language's lexicon is the total number of words that can be combined grammatically to form primary meaning units, called sentences or propositions.

Each language is used by an identifiable group of people (a language group), but it can also be translated into other languages, because meaning is a universal human value. However, each language divides human experience in a distinctive way. As a result the surface structure of no two languages is exactly the same. Thus, there cannot be an exact word-for-word translation of the Greek New Testament that would be idiomatic English. To understand a literary work in any language, a reader needs linguistic competence in that symbolic system, that is, knowledge of its vocabulary, grammar, semantic network and pragmatic rules.

Members of one language group can learn an unfamiliar language, even one that is no longer spoken, like Hellenistic Greek. This process involves mastering a variety of skills. Because most contemporary Christians do not have the opportunity to become familiar with New Testament Greek, I have prepared this linguistic introduction to make a reading of the canon or normative liturgical library of the Christian Church more intelligible. This book will point out features of both content and structure that will be helpful in understanding the 27 short writings or "books" of the New Testament.

In a sense modern readers must enter into a process similar to the one that native Greek speakers undertook when they encountered the writings of the early Christians, who really spoke a new language. It is a process of gaining facility in this new language world. One dimension that must be added by modern readers is transcultural awareness, because every language participates in the culture of its users. The science that studies the interaction of a language and its culture is called sociolinguistics. Obviously, it is difficult to become familiar with the culture of the world of the New Testament, and biblical scholars are only at the beginning stage in developing methods to do so. This book will touch on some of the features of sociolinguistics in Chapter 12.

Example. Matt 13: 24-52. The Gospel of Matthew groups together a series of parables about "the Kingdom of Heaven." The image of the Kingdom of God is common to all three Synoptic Gospels. Matthew's substitution of the term "Heaven" for "God" reflects the practice of Jews at the time of Jesus to refrain from pronouncing the divine name and to substitute another term.

The following chapters of Part I will deal with the mechanics of how language works and illustrate the principles by examples from the New Testament.

Sources

Fitzgerald, John J., 1966, *Peirce's Theory of Signs as Foundation for Pragmatism.* The Hague: Mouton.

Jakobson, Roman, 1978, *Six Lectures on Sound and Meaning.* Cambridge: MIT Press.

Kopesec, Michael F., 1982, "Bilingualism and the Assessment of Translation Needs," *Notes on Translation* 88: 2-18.

Nida, Eugene A., 1975, *Componential Analysis of Meaning.* The Hague: Mouton.

Oller, John W., 1972, "On the Relation between Syntax, Semantics and Pragmatics," *Linguistics* 83: 43-55.

Peirce, Charles S., 1931-1958, *Collected Papers*, edited by Charles Hartshorne and Paul Weiss. Cambridge: Harvard U. Press.

Wilder, Amos N. ,1971, *Early Christian Rhetoric: The Language of the Gospels*. Reissue. Cambridge: Harvard U. Press.

Chapter 2

The Complexity of Words

As an oral-aural, that is, speaking-hearing system of symbols, a language is built upon oppositions, the interplay of variants and invariants in its sound system. All aspects of this complex system of networks mentioned in Chapter 1 form part of the meaning effect of language. Every language then is a stratified system with surface and depth levels. But the surface or grammatical relations of the words correlate only loosely with the meaning of the sentence (proposition) as a whole, that is, with its semantic level.

To grasp the meaning of any writings — and especially an ancient text like the New Testament — readers must analyze its surface form and compare that network with its semantic level or meaning kernels. The surface form of each language is unique, but all languages have similar meaning kernels. Thus, meaning is found not so much in individual words, which in themselves have rather "meaning potential" than meaning, as in the way words are related in context. These relationships make up the discourse structure of a text. The discourse structure embraces a hierarchy of elements: words, phrases, clauses, sentences, paragraphs, sections, chapters, ultimately the entire discourse as a unified literary whole. The entire work forms the context for understanding each element in it. These more general units of meaning will be treated in the discussion of discourse analysis in Chapters 4-6.

Within propositions or sentences, meaning embraces not only the informational content but all forms of experience and emotion that are part of the communication event or speech act. The next chapter will be devoted to the communication event. This chapter will focus on words (technically called lexemes in linguistics). Within a text words play three roles at the same time: 1) grammatical — as nouns, verbs, adjectives and other parts of speech; 2) syntactical — as subject, predicate, direct object and other parts of a sentence; 3) semantic — as having a meaning effect. Because the meaning effect of words is so important in understanding the New Testament, the following section will explain the componential analysis of words.

Universal Semantic Domains of Words. In all languages words can be divided into four universal classes or domains of meaning, that is, into four primary kernels of meaning:

1) things or objects: names of persons, places and other entities that usually appear as nouns in the surface structure.

2) events: actions, processes, activities, states of being that usually appear as verbs in the surface structure.

Example. Rom 1:8 speaks of the "faith" of the recipients. As a part of speech "faith" is a noun but semantically it is not an object. Rather it designates the process or activity of entrusting their life to God.

3) abstracts: which are qualities of both things and events, showing their extent, quantity or intensity. In most cases abstracts take the form of adjectives or adverbs.

4) relationals: a special kind of functional abstracts that are significant enough to merit distinct semantic treatment.

Relationals ordinarily take the form of conjunctions or prepositions, but they also appear as interjections and sentences particles. At times demonstratives and personal adjectives fulfill this role because they point to the variety of relationships affecting a person. For example, the term "my" indicates a variety of relations when used with such nouns as soul, husband, song, voice, house, debt.

Example. Rom 1:1, 9. The phrases "gospel of God" and "gospel of his Son." The "of," which translates the Greek genitive case, speaks of two different relationships between the two nouns in each expression. In the first phrase, God is the author and originator of the gospel as way of salvation. In the second case, the Son is subject and agent who makes the gospel available to believers.

Within these universal semantic domains are smaller classifications of words into related fields or categories (see Chapter 10). The exact meaning of the word in any context can be discovered by placing it in its appropriate word field. Some words are a combination of meanings from more than one semantic domain. For example, a "messiah" encompasses three semantic categories: as a person (domain of thing) who has been anointed (domain of action) for a role (domain of process). The word "repentance" in itself is a turning (domain of action) but it implies a previous condition of being a sinner (domain of state of being) and the adopting of a new kind of life (domain of state of being).

Semantic domains are not limited to communicating the informational content of a word. As verbal symbols words exercise meaning effect in a variety of other ways, like emotive, figurative, logical and encyclopedic. Some of the more important types of meaning involved in understanding the New Testament are:

1) cognitive. This is the conceptual element. It designates the diagnostic features that identify the semantic domain to which the word points. When I say that the cognitive domain is diagnostic, I mean that it analyzes distinctive features of words to put them into their logical categories. In natural languages the link between the form of the word and the object to which it refers is arbitrary and conventional. Thus, there is no intrinsic reason why the green plant used to compose lawns should be called "grass." In fact, this same plant has hundreds of different names according to the

language in which the concept is found.

2) emotive. This is the connotation implied by a term. Languages often have a variety of words for the same object or event. Some of these are found in formal settings, others in scientific writing, others in conversation or slang. Some terms are excluded from accepted social exchange, such as words that convey ethnic and racial prejudice.

Example. Matt 15:26. When Jesus quotes the popular proverb about not giving the food of children to "dogs," he is using an emotive term the Jews used to express their disdain for pagans.

3) figurative. This is a metaphorical use of words, based on an extension of their cognitive meaning. The ability of words to be semantically stretched creates the possibility of that great variety of figures of speech that make languages colorful (see Chapter 9). Usually figurative meanings are related closely to the particular culture of a language group. For this reason figurative usage is often difficult to translate, and New Testament readers today may misunderstand the thrust of figurative expressions.

Example. Luke 13:32. When Jesus hears that Herod wants to kill him, he refers to Herod as a "fox," a figurative expression in Hellenistic Greek for a crafty person.

4) encyclopedic. The objects to which words refer often have a variety of additional features that are not essential to determining their meaning, but which can be helpful in identifying a concrete form. These features make up the encyclopedic information ordinarily listed in dictionaries. It is important to remember that all of these qualities are not designated or implied each time a word is used. Only the context indicates to readers the focus and set of relations that an individual word conveys in any particular instance. To try to read all possible meanings of a word into its every use is a faulty method called "totality transfer" that leads to a distortion of meaning (Louw: 42).

Eugene Nida, for many years Translations Research Coordinator for the United Bible Societies, has often explained the various qualities words have as linguistic symbols (Nida: 47-53). Among these are:

1) except for proper names, words refer not to individual items but to classes of referents, which may be large or small.

2) words are arbitrary and receive their meanings by common convention. They are constantly subject to expansion, contraction and shifts in focus. They may drop out of usage or take on additional meaning potential. In brief, words are territories of meaning.

3) words operate within a social context which has its own dynamism and interrelationships. In such a setting they provide adequate means for communicating human experience.

4) various users often employ words from a different focus. Because they understand words from their own backgrounds, perfect intelligibility is never achieved. Yet a high level of mutual understanding is possible in verbal communication.

Example. 2 Cor 4:13-14. Paul expresses his confidence that he can communicate in preaching the message of faith he received.

In addition to explaining the meaning effect or meaning potential of individual words, semantics deals with other dimensions of communication, such as: 1) how meaning is realized in both linguistic and nonlinguistic context; 2) the meaning at every level of discourse, that is, within groups of words, between groups of words, between sentences, paragraphs and larger discourse units; 3) the process of translation, which is the transfer of meaning between languages. What can be said in one language can be said at least substantially in others, if not always as economically or elegantly. The surface form will often change and nuances of meaning may be lost, but readers in the receptor language will be able to grasp the substance of meaning if the text is well translated.

Two principal methods of translation exist: formal and dynamic equivalent. The formal method tries to reproduce the form or surface structure of the original text. Thus a formal translation reads like an imitation of the original language and it is often stilted. By contrast, in dynamic equivalent translation the key is the technique of semantic paraphrase. Semantic paraphrase transforms the surface structure of the text into its semantic kernels — sometimes called its deep structure — and then transfers these meaning kernels into the grammatical structure of the receptor language. This method, developed by Eugene Nida, was employed in translating *Good News for Modern Man* and influenced the American Catholic translation, the *New American Bible* (Reese: 21-22).

Sources

Louw, J. P., 1982, *Semantics of New Testament Greek.* Phila.: Fortress.

Nida, Eugene A., 1975, *Language Structure and Translation: Essays.* Stanford: Stanford University Press.

Reese, James M., 1975, *Preaching God's Burning Word.* Collegeville: Liturgical Press.

Chapter 3

Linguistic Interaction:
The Communication Event

Any approach to interpreting the New Testament must keep aware that none of its 27 books was meant to be an abstract aesthetic object created to be contemplated in a vacuum. All were written because the community needed instruction, guidance, encouragement.

Example. 2 Tim 3:16 speaks of the practical role of all Scripture. This statement refers to the Jewish Scriptures but can also be applied to the New Testament canon, the normative writings of the Christian community, produced by that community. In addition, the Church accepts as canonical the Jewish Scriptures and some intertestamental writings as its Old Testament, but this study is not directly concerned with them.

Language is for communication. Each act of communication is unique because the total situation of the exchange can never be repeated exactly. A theory of how language communicates belongs to pragmatics, which treats of the setting and interconnection of the communication process. In his lectures, published posthumously under the title of

How to Do Things with Words, J. L. Austin developed a theory of how words do things. This approach was further developed and modified by linguists such as John R. Searle in terms of the various relationships, effects and intentions involved in verbal communication.

The most common approach to speech acts discusses them in terms of:

a) locutionary acts (also called propositional acts): the producing of some form of meaning by structuring words.

b) illocutionary acts: a name for all those language compositions that are aimed at behavioral modification. The aim of speech is not merely to utter meaning but to be meaningful, that is, to involve choice. Why this instead of that? Searle lists five types of illocutionary acts: assertives, directives, commissives, expressives and declaratives.

c) perlocutionary acts: those specific occasions when an utterance actually effects a behavioral change, such as annoying a hearer or getting a reader to vote.

Roman Jakobson worked out another approach to speech acts, which I call "communication events" in this book, because I am concerned with written texts. He developed a twofold scheme to explain the elements of language that function in human communication. His writings place the emphasis on practical dimensions in using language as a medium of communication. His analysis has been modified by a few linguists, but it is widely accepted as a fruitful model for actually using language as the primary vehicle for human communication. I find it more helpful for this study than the philosophical approach of Austin.

New Testament authors kept in touch with the oral preaching out of which the Christian Church grew. Their writings can be studied as a series of communication events each of which contributed to forming the canonical texts that continue to serve as the basis for the Christian community's worship and social communication. This chapter will describe first the six factors and then the six functions that Jakobson saw as comprising the network of human language communication.

THE SIX FACTORS OF A COMMUNICATION EVENT

1. *Sender*. Whether as speaker or author, the originator of a message initiates communication to have some effect in society, such as making information available or revealing a personal response to some stimulus.

Example. Gal 1:6-10. Paul expresses amazement at the fickleness of the Galatians in turning away from the good news of salvation as he had preached it to them.

2. *Message*. It is as an artistic creation in verbal form that the text becomes a vehicle of communication between sender and recipients. It thus becomes an independent entity and is subject to analysis and commentary according to principles of literary criticism.

Example. The Letter to Philemon. This is a short letter that the apostle Paul wrote from prison. It is composed to lead Philemon to adopt a certain mode of acting toward his runaway slave Onesimus.

3. *Addressees*. The intended audience of a piece of verbal communication can be either present or absent. A written communication is addressed to potential reading audiences that can decode the message at any time. In itself, the written text never changes, but it can become obscure or unintelligible to its potential audience because of changes in culture. This is the situation of New Testament writings, which require transcultural interpretation. They must be interpreted for modern Western audiences who are not familiar with the original context of the writings.

Example. Hebrews 9:1-5. The passage mentions details of the sacred shrine of Israel. These items are foreign and meaningless to most contemporary American readers.

4. *Context*. Every message originates in a concrete situation that is shared by the sender and the original audience. This common context specifies the meaning of the words and how detailed descriptions have to be.

Example. 1 Cor 7-15. In the second part of First Corinthians Paul responds to questions sent to him by that community. He does not repeat the questions before responding. Modern readers, not knowing either the questions or the context, have difficulty in understanding the force of Paul's reasoning or the reason for the dilemmas faced by the original audience.

5. *Contact*. The intended audience must hear the message. In addition to actual physical contact with the sound in spoken communication, contact includes psychological ability to receive the message. To achieve contact with the New Testament, modern readers must first of all be part of the long network of textual history that has preserved the text. Second, for those reading it in their own language rather than in Greek, the accuracy of translation is necessary for contact with the text.

Example. Mark 4:10-12. This is a comment on the effect that the message of Jesus had on diverse groups. It refers to the psychological contact demanded for hearing the parables of Jesus. That contact is the humility and openness of heart to hear their call to conversion.

6.*Code*. Every message is delivered in an identifiable language. Potential readers must know the vocabulary and syntax sufficiently to grasp the message.

Example. Rev 6:1-17. This narrates a vision written in the stylized code of Jewish apocalyptic. To understand the vision, the reader must be familiar with the code, which involves biblical symbols.

THE SIX FUNCTIONS OF A COMMUNICATION EVENT

Jakobson also finds six functions involved in the communication act. Other commentators differ on the number and on their names or on specific roles of the individual functions that he suggests. The following list follows Jakobson but notes other suggestions. In addition, individual languages may divide these functions in different ways because the functions do not correspond exactly to the factors of communication acts. All the functions describe how the factors interact in a specific instance of communication. When the communication takes place by writing, the text eventually assumes primacy when the author is no longer present to clarify difficulties. Moreover, authors never have perfect control of language and cannot make it achieve all and only what they intend. Hence, although every attempt must be made to respect an author's intention, that is only one factor in interpreting. Commentators must carefully analyze the text as written to grasp its meaning.

Readers must tear a text apart linguistically to grasp a message with all the communication events found in it. The following remarks about the functions of communication events deal with written texts because this book is concerned with contributing to a fuller understanding of the New Testament. Its authors chose literary forms and vocabulary conformable to the prevailing traditions that they wished to pass on. In Chapter 8 further attention will be given to language artistry.

1. *Emotive*, also called evaluative or appraisive function. This is the function of the text that communicates the dimension of an experience that goes beyond information or conceptual content. It is what the text conveys of emotion or insight or value. In oral delivery the tone of voice and animation of delivery convey emotion. In writing it must be shared by rhetorical features, all that makes up style. Psycholinguists devise tests to measure the emotive impact of a text.

Examples. Luke 18:8. The rhetorical question conveys the emotion of Jesus as he sees a lack of faith. Romans 9-11. Paul shares his personal experience as a member of the Jewish religion who has embraced faith in Jesus Christ. His emotive description of God's plan of salvation conveys the overwhelming impact of the power of the gospel on him.

2. *Poetic* "Poetic" here is used in the Greek sense of "creative." It means the impact of a text as a literary creation. Every text is an artificial construct, a creation to be received as a literary unity. The artistry of each part — from individual sentences to the structured whole — depends upon the choice of vocabulary and the kinds of figures employed. Modern studies on discourse analysis, that is, on how texts are structured, aid in appreciating the poetic dimension of the message.

Example. The Gospel of Mark can be studied as story. This approach explains the impact of its structure and the interaction of its characters in conveying the mission of Jesus.

3. *Evocative*, also called imperative, prescriptive, provocative, persuasive or conative (because it appeals for a response) function. The evocative function is the one most closely linked to an author's style. Hence, ability to resonate to literary features like irony, metaphor and understatement is an important condition for appreciating the evocative function of a text. Yet, readers hear a text against a variety of backgrounds: their cultural and religious traditions, their personal expectations, needs, agenda. What effect a communication event has upon them may be determined more by their own situation and feelings than by the intention of the author.

Reader response criticism has called attention to the importance of the evocative function by explaining the active role of a reader in interpreting the messages encoded in a text (Eco). This feature will be discussed in Chapter 7. Since every text is a "texture," it unfolds a variety of messages at the same time. In fact, that is how Christian commentators from Patristic times on have read Scripture and applied it to the changing conditions of the Church and the world.

Examples. 2 Peter 1:20-21 speaks of the activity on the part of the Holy Spirit as needed to interpret prophecy. In 1 Cor 1:4-9, Paul makes an ironic allusion to the boasting of the Corinthians about their spiritual gifts. He is seeking to evoke the wisdom of the Spirit in them.

4. *Referential* or denotative; also called informative, cognitive or descriptive function. It refers to how the text deals with the subject matter being treated. Every text says something about something or someone. Even fiction narrates events about characters that are a real creation of an author in their own world. The referential meaning is a "bundle of conceptual features which set off the referential potential of such a unit from all other units of language" (Nida: 203).

Example. 2 Cor 8:1 — 9:15 refers to the collection that Paul is supervising for the Christian community of Jerusalem, which is suffering because of a severe famine.

5. *Phatic*. This function consists of those features of a text that serve to keep communication open with readers. A skillful author builds this function into the text to compensate for the absence of tone of voice and other features of oral style.

Example. In 1 Thess 1:2-10, a thanksgiving prayer, Paul brings hearers (and eventually readers) into his world of faith. By this thanksgiving Paul creates a liturgical setting. He forges new bonds of communication with the members of this young community to whom he writes as founding apostle.

6. *Metalinguistic*. This function flows out of the nature of language as a code. It is the exploiting of the power of language as a sign system to comment upon itself — as is done in teaching grammar or learning a second language. This function is common in technical treatises on language but rarely appears in literary writing.

Example. Gal 3:16. Paul interprets the singular form of the Greek noun "seed" in Genesis 12:7; 17:7 as referring explicitly to Jesus rather than as being an abstract term for descendants in general.

The above description of communication events based on the analysis of Roman Jakobson covers straightforward situations adequately. But, because of sophisticated techniques also found, I want to look at complicated communication situations in the next chapter.

Sources

Austin, J. L., 1962, *How to Do Things with Words*. Oxford: Oxford University Press.

Eco, Umberto, 1979, *The Role of the Reader: Explorations in the Semiotics of Texts*. Bloomington: Indiana U. Press.

Jakobson, Roman, 1960, "Closing Statements: Linguistics and Poetics," in T.A. Sebeok, ed., *Style in Language*. Cambridge: MIT Press. Reprinted in *Selected Writings* 3:18-51. The Hague: Mouton, 1981.

Nida, Eugene A., 1975, *Componential Analysis of Meaning*. The Hague: Mouton.

Pratt, Mary Louise, 1977, *Toward a Speech Act Theory of Literary Discourse*. Bloomington: Indiana U. Press.

Searle, John R., 1979, *Expression and Meaning: Studies on the Theory of Speech Acts*. NY: Cambridge U. Press.

Chapter 4

What Is Said and What Is Meant: Complicated Communication Situations

Speech act or communication event theory explains the variety of activities performed in speaking: naming, describing, informing, questioning, commanding, confusing, stirring up emotions, thanking, and so forth. However, a speaker may say one thing and mean another, either to deceive or to use language artistically.

Example. Matt 2:8. Herod told the magi to return to him when they found the baby so that he could also go and "adore" — a misuse of the term. James 3:6 figuratively describes the tongue as a fire ignited by Gehenna, a term equivalent to hell in Jewish folklore.

Communication events are complex and reveal their total conceptual and emotive meaning only when they are analyzed to determine the types of activities involved. As noted in Chapter 3, over and above the physical act of making a sound, speech acts fall into one of three levels: 1) locutionary — what kind of statement is made in respect to the truth content. How appropriate is the utterance? 2) illocutionary — what kind of communication event is performed, like informing or questioning. 3) perlocutionary — insofar as the speech act produces its intended effect.

Examples. The New Testament records certain performative speech acts of Jesus. Matt 8:13. Jesus speaks and the child is cured. John 18:6. When Jesus says, "I am," the crowd falls back, overpowered by the impact of his words.

As shown in Chapter 3, for an analysis of simple communication acts the division of Roman Jakobson is most helpful. However, in many texts they are not confined to a pure type and their functions overlap. Hence, before looking at some complicated communication situations in the New Testament, it will be helpful to elaborate briefly the categories of speech acts listed by John Searle. (They are simplified somewhat):

1) assertives (or representatives) — to represent or describe a referent or topic spoken about, that is, to make statements or to ask informational questions.

2) expressives — to convey a speaker's will or feeling, such as gratitude or sorrow.

3) commissives — to involve or commit the speaker in some action, as in promising to help or in blessing.

4) directives or emotives — to move hearers to a change of behavior, as in commands, requests, prayers and rhetorical questions.

These types constitute the main semantic dimensions of language as it functions in communicating. In practice, however, speakers in all languages often communicate their meaning in a disguised way. A skewing of levels occurs because the surface or grammatical form differs from the semantic kernel intended. What is meant is not directly apparent from what is said. This discrepancy is part of style, the rhetorical side of language. Native speakers deal with this feature of language without difficulty, but it has become the subject of a full-scale debate in the movement known as "deconstruction." "Illocutionary force does not necessarily follow from grammatical structure" (Culler: 113).

Example. Matt 7:16. In asking the rhetorical question whether persons gather figs from thorns, Jesus is not seeking information but is conveying a directive. He invites hearers to investigate the sincerity of their behavior.

When communication events are disguised in any way, the ingenuity of readers is called into play. They must coordinate the surface and the semantic levels of the text (what the sentence means) with the pragmatic flow (how it communicates). For example, when the driver of an automobile says, "Would you like to fasten your seat belts?" passengers know that this is a command, not a question. From the context, hearers can adjust the surface form to what the driver really means. Such indirect communication events are similar on the discourse level to idioms in the realm of vocabulary. They do not reveal their meaning by logical analysis but must be dealt with in the sociolinguistic setting. This is a cultural aspect of language. An important dimension of this conventional nature of language is technically known as "implicature." Implicature involves "aspects of the conveyed message of the utterance which are distinct from its truth conditional meaning" (Thomson: 2).

In complex statements many things are implied that are not overtly stated. Native speakers are habitually aware of them and take them for granted — or rather, know how to integrate them in their understanding of the text. But readers from another culture are not aware of them and easily misunderstand implications of polite forms and other indirections.

Example. John 2:4. In the Greek text the words of Jesus to his mother read literally, "Woman, what to me and to thee?" No translator keeps this phrase exactly because all recognize that it is an idiom with certain implications. The problem is to determine exactly what is implied.

FURTHER COMPLICATIONS IN LANGUAGE MAKE-UP

It is becoming increasingly evident that the analysis of how language functions is extremely complicated. This is why linguists have developed a variety of ways to approach the task of interpretation. It challenges them at every level of discourse, beginning with the morpheme, which is the smallest semantic or meaning unit recognized by linguists, (like re-ply in contrast to re-lie), and continuing on to the understanding of the entire text as a unity. Every step of the process is interrelated because, in some sense, every word contains the whole discourse in germ, and every discourse is a complex word-sign.

At the same time, as a behavioral event no discourse can possess all meaning. Its meaning is linked to the shared perceptions of the participants in the communication event. Here some additional comment is needed about the kinds of roles words and idioms perform in textual communication. The roles are related to the arbitrary nature of linguistic signs explained in Chapter 1.

Example. John 4:9 comments that Jews did not "use common vessels" with Samaritans. A study of the use of this expression among Hellenistic authors indicates that it was a way of saying that two groups did not associate. It means more than it says.

Eugene Nida's collection of articles on language structure and meaning are helpful in understanding the New Testament. He stresses that commentators must focus attention on the semantic structure of language rather than on referents of words for three reasons: first, the relationship of the verbal sign to the referent is arbitrary. Readers must become aware of how the sign performs in specific contexts; second, in each language experience is broken up in different ways into arbitrary segments; third, no consistent relation exists between meaning classes of words and referent classes. In other words, the meaning of a word cannot be known from its formal structure.

All these complications demand that interpreters discover the way the fundamental semantic units of the Hellenistic Greek used in the New Testament function. Four important guides to follow are:

1. The basic unit may be either a morpheme or a word. A morpheme is the smallest unit with meaning potential. It can be a part of a word that is found only in conjunction with other parts, as the English morpheme "-pare" in words like compare. At times these morphemes provide the basis for puns, plays on words and comparisons that are often lost in translation.

Example. 2 Thess 3:11 compares those who conduct themselves irresponsibly by not working (*ergazomenous*) but by minding other peoples' business (*periergazomenous*)

2. Idioms act as a single meaning unit. An idiom is an exocentric unit, that is, its meaning is in a combination of terms rather than in any single one of them. For example, in English, the fact that "a can of worms" means a difficult situation does not come from any single term in the expression but from the whole. In fact, none of the individual terms gives a hint of the meaning of the idiom.

Example. Mark 2:10 (and almost 100 other places in the four gospels) Jesus refers to "the Son of (the) man," an idiomatic expression whose meaning is not equivalent to the words individually.

Other idioms deal with the range of distribution of the terms, such as: what adjectives may be used with this noun? to what kind of situation does this term apply? Thus, English speaks of "a sweet tooth," but not of a sweet mouth. Some idioms have specific emotional connotation.

Example. Heb 7:9 contains an archaic classical phrase meaning "to use the right word," which gives the passage a solemn tone.

3. The semantic unit may be a unitary complex, that is, two words in a phrase may designate a single referent which is different from the principal noun, as in "greenhouse."

Example. John 20:22. In the phrase, "Receive the Holy Spirit," Jesus promises a distinct personal communication of divine power who will work in and among his followers. In this combination, "Spirit" takes on a significance that does not belong to the term in ordinary (technically called "unmarked") usage.

4. The meaning or semantic unit may be a special composite, that is, a new term created by modifying another word.

Example. Heb 5:1. The term "high priest" in the Greek text is a compound word that designates a special class of priests. It is applied to Jesus to designate his unique role as mediator.

Individual words and communication events can be complex, but their complexity is multiplied when they are joined into continuous discourse. The next three chapters will introduce readers into recent research on discourse analysis.

Sources

Culler, Jonathan, 1982, *On Deconstruction: Theory and Criticism after Structuralism*. Ithaca: Cornell U. Press.

Nida, Eugene A., 1975, *Language Structure and Meaning*. Stanford: Stanford U. Press.

Polythress, Vern S., 1979, "Analysing a Biblical Text: Some Important Linguistic Distinctions," *Scottish Journal of Theology* 32:113-137.

Searle, John R., 1969, *Speech Acts*. Cambridge: Cambridge U. Press

Thomson, Greg, 1982, "An Introduction to Implicature for Translators," *Notes on Translation*: Special Edition, January.

Chapter 5

Discourse Analysis I:
Authorial Intention

Up to this point discussion has centered around the meaning potential of words: how do words mean when they are combined into propositions or sentences? But the meaning of individual sentences is only a small part of understanding New Testament writings. A text is an organization of sentences grouped into units of increasing complexity. In expository writing the units are paragraphs, chapters, sections, whole work. In narratives and dramas the units include scenes and episodes.

That part of literary criticism that studies principles governing the flow of thought and action throughout a text is called discourse analysis, an area that has attracted the attention of linguists in recent years. It is this part of interpretation or hermeneutics that Louw refers to when he writes, "Semantics is more than the meaning of words" (Louw: 91).

On the widest level, the meaning of a text is the unique result achieved by uniting specific content to a particular form. All the elements of a communication event in written form are involved in this process, which brings together three participants: author, text and readers. This discussion starts with the role of the author because any question about the meaning of a literary work must begin with what the author set out to accomplish. We can assume that every New Testament author — including the writer of the Apocalypse — wrote to communicate. "Hence, the speaker's meaning and the discourse meaning were, for the most part, quite close if not virtually identical" (Polythress: 123).

Extending the context further back in time, a text has its origins before it is written, namely, in a semiotic or linguistic tradition. Individual authors create a text only in the sense of being interpreters of other texts and traditions, linguistic or nonlinguistic. Each author works with a set of signs developed by a language group for mutual communication. What the author does is to choose and arrange the language resources available in a way appropriate to represent a new situation. From an analysis of the resulting text, it is possible to make judgments about the nature of a particular discourse as well as about the purpose of its author.

Such judgments must always remain tentative because the possibilities of using and misusing and distorting language are infinitely diverse. Some possibilities are: 1) an author can be sidetracked or confused and so fail to produce the intended result; 2) an author may not be in perfect command of a language and so produce a text that is ambiguous or unclear; 3) an author may be malicious and prepare a deceitful text.

Critics are still in the process of drawing up rules to describe and distinguish the unfolding of discourse as distinct from individual sentences. As yet no single system of terms to identify its various functions is universally accepted. The following division of discourse types is not meant to be exhaustive. Rather, it is geared to the significant kinds of discourse found in the New Testament:

1) Declarative or informative discourse — to make known information that conforms to reality and so will be helpful in influencing the behaviorial choices of readers.

Example. 1 Cor 11:23-27. Paul informs his readers of the institution of the Eucharist by Jesus and makes clear its significance for their sanctification.

2) Imperative discourse — to communicate intentionality in a way that is calculated to bring recipients to conform their actions to a goal.

Example. 1 Cor 6:17-20. Paul directs his readers toward conforming to the sexual integrity demanded of members of Christ.

3) Performative discourse. In certain publically structured situations (as that of judges in a court or betters at a race track) authorized speakers effect a change by the very uttering of certain words. "I find you guilty." "I bet $50."

Example. Mark 3:14-16. Jesus in virtue of his sense of mission appoints and thereby empowers the Twelve to be with him and to preach the Kingdom and to expel demons.

4) Assertive discourse. Authors can structure a text so that it does not merely describe their belief but communicates their commitment to a certain course of action by virtue of it.

Example. John 6:32-40. In this part of his Bread of Life discourse, Jesus affirms commitment to his Father and to the revelation of his Father's will for him.

5) Emotive discourse — a text organized not to communicate concepts but to express a writer's emotions.

Example. Acts 19:33-40. Alexander the Jew expresses fear of the harm that could come from this uprising.

These examples illustrate intentions expressed either by writers of New Testament books themselves or by speakers whom they record. Obviously authors may have multiple intentions in composing; so it is not always possible to be specific in affirming authorial intention by a superficial reading of a text. As pointed out in Chapter 4, in some cases authors write something different from what they intend to convey. This situation occurs especially when they use rhetorical figures, which will be treated in Chapter 8. They demand special reader involvement.

Psycholinguists attempt to investigate the relation of the text to the preconscious and the unconscious as part of the process of isolating authorial intention. That is a new and still uncharted dimension of semantic research which calls for more specialized treatment than this book offers.

Technically speaking, the approach to discourse analysis that is being explained in these three chapters is an exercise of semiotics. It is based on the insights of Charles S. Peirce as developed by linguists like Roman Jakobson. "The contemporary semiotics of literature is founded on Jakobson's work" (Scholes: xii). Peirce's important insight was that signs can be defined only by other signs. The total sign system is operative in the network of social communication, only one aspect of which is to link referents to specific signs in the variety of ways mentioned above. Semiotics is needed to prevent language from being reduced to a theory of knowledge that equates meaning with reference. It not only encourages a comprehensive approach to interpretation but helps to integrate insights from the variety of methods that operate in the contemporary language explosion.

Sources

Louw, J. P., 1982, *Semantics of New Testament Greek*. Phila.: Fortress.

Polythress, Vern S., 1979, "Analysing a Biblical Text: Some Important Linguistic Distinctions," *Scottish Journal of Theology* 32:113-137.

Ricoeur, Paul, 1974, "The Question of Subject: The Challenge of Semiology," *The Conflict of Interpretations*. Evanston: Northwestern U. Press, 236-266.

Scholes, Robert, 1982, *Semiotics and Interpretation*. New Haven: Yale U. Press.

Searle, John R., 1979, *Expression and Meaning: Studies in the Theory of Speech Acts*. NY: Cambridge U. Press.

Chapter 6

Discourse Analysis II: Structuring a Text

Every discourse proposes to be an organic series of communication events. That is why the author's intentionality must be the starting point for discourse analysis; no one sends a message without some purpose. At the same time, an individual author is not the ultimate source of the entire discourse. Every text prolongs, interprets and comments upon previous texts and traditions in the system of verbal signs shared by the linguistic community. Hence the next step in explaining discourse analysis is to examine varieties of literary expression — the categories that underline specific literary genres available to the New Testament authors.

As in the case of the grammatical and semantic classification of individual verbal forms (discussed in Chapter 2), various possibilities for classification of discourse are available. But additional factors enter into the task of analyzing structured texts. Readers approach a text with their own expectations, which are shaped by their knowledge and evaluation of the category to which it belongs. The entire text is both context and instrument by which readers choose the meaning of every element in its unfolding. When a large amount of material is to be communicated, that is, when a long text is needed, structure or form should assume a supportive role. But that is not always the case. For example, if the structure of such a piece is transparent, the work can be monotonous and boring. But if the structure is unclear or confused, readers easily get lost.

On the other hand, if a text is short — as with proverbs and many other wisdom pieces — the sociolinguistic background is extremely important for readers (Tannehill). Their ability to interpret depends to a large extent on knowing how the speech community made use of such forms. When short pieces are imbedded in a longer piece, the whole text gives them special focus.

Examples. Luke 18:1, 9. By directing the parable to a specific audience, Luke suggests its thrust. Matt 8:22. Jesus answers a wavering disciple with a traditional proverb. Its interpretation is influenced by the fact that this vocation scene is embedded in a series of ten miracle stories.

WAYS OF DIVIDING DISCOURSE

An adequate division of the types of discourse demands some clear distinction between viewing the text as a whole (a unified literary work) and viewing the components that are used in its composition. Eugene Nida calls these two approaches macrorhetoric and microrhetoric. Macrorhetoric deals with those forces that shape discourse as a literary whole; microrhetoric is concerned with the figurative use of language, especially figures of speech.

In this relatively new area of research, linguists do not agree on a single approach for dividing a discourse into categories. Since a language is an open-ended system and in constant flux, any categories are subject to refinement. The following approach is directed toward interpreting the kinds of discourse found in the New Testament. The general thrust follows the approach of Nida, who divides discourse according to the ways in which movement proceeds in them:

1) Temporal progress. This type of discourse appears in the category of narrative or story. It treats characters as acting within the framework of the past. A story does not have to be told in strictly chronological order and may use a first person or third person narrator. The narrator may be a character in the story or an all-pervading, all-knowing figure who can reveal even unvoiced thoughts of characters. A story does not aim at historical completeness but focuses in on those actions of characters that advance the plot. Traditionally, stories have moved toward a climax, but modern narratives may simply string together a series of scenes. "By narrative we seek to orient ourselves in our experience of temporal succession and memory" (Wilder: 360).

Example. The infancy narratives of Matthew and Luke use two different types of story. Matthew links scenes to texts from Jewish Scripture; Luke contrasts the story of Jesus and John.

As stories embedded in the Synoptic Gospels, the parables of Jesus have a distinct narrative form, although they are artistic creations. The question of the historicity of narratives must be kept distinct from their religious message, which is communicated by the interaction between elements of the story as story.

2) Progress in space. This form of discourse may deal with progress through physical space or with location in figurative space, like lists, which is an ancient discourse form. Both forms are descriptions. The contents they describe may be discrete physical objects or abstract qualities. Descriptions prescind from time. They concentrate on the how of the topic: how do these items appear and interrelate?

Examples. The New Testament has several lists, such as virtues and vices. Gal 5:19-21 lists the works of the "flesh," and Gal 5:22-23 names the fruits of the Spirit. Heb 9:1-5 lists objects in the sanctuary of the Temple of Jerusalem.

3) Logical progress. When a discourse proceeds along logical lines, it is called an exposition. No particular charac-

ters or time periods are involved because expository discourse defines, explains or interprets. Language offers a variety of forms for expository discourse: for example, expressions of dependence like cause and effect; explanations of qualification like showing the manner in which an action took place; explanations of relationship, like comparison and contrast. Since its goal is to explain how items are linked logically, exposition deals with specifics and demands clarity. Unity is usually achieved by selecting a theme and developing it in a coherent fashion. This development may be the unpacking of a topic sentence in carefully chosen terms. Or the author may develop the theme gradually by working toward a climax.

Some paragraphs of exposition even use a question and answer format, or construe an imaginary dialog form — a feature of the diatribe, which is a philosophical polemic. Other rhetorical devices that can enliven exposition include illustrations, examples and the use of models. Some recent New Testament commentators call attention to the flow of discourse in an expository writing like the Letter to the Romans. That approach shows more sensitivity to the role of discourse analysis than an introduction that merely lists the content of the letter.

Examples. In Rom 5:12-21 Paul explains how sin entered the world through the sin of Adam and how the grace of Christ overcomes sin. In 1 Cor 1:13 Paul asks three rhetorical questions, which he proceeds to answer in reverse order. These three questions thus provide his original recipients (who would be hearing the letter read in Corinth) with an outline of the flow of the first part of his reply to their confusion. Gal 3:1-6 uses the diatribe method to advance the discourse. The First Letter of John illustrates a Semitic style of exposition, a circular style portraying God as light, as just and as love.

4) Exhortation or progress from one attitude to another. This form of discourse aims at arousing response in those who are addressed. They are usually commanded or exhorted in the direct second person address. However, for

variation in style, those addressed may be designated by titles, such as "beloved" or "brothers." Exhortation is sometimes classified as a form of logical progression, but it differs in focus from exposition: 1) because its specific goal is to effect a change in activity; 2) because it offers motives for pursuing a course of action in contrast to providing an explanation of how to achieve the goal. In the New Testament Greek text, the imperative form will dominate but it may be replaced by other grammatical forms like the subjunctive or future vivid.

Examples. New Testament letters usually have a section devoted to exhortation after an exposition of an aspect of Christian teaching. Thus, 1 Thess 5:14-22 is a set of staccato commands. The Letter to the Hebrews alternates between exposition and exhortation, which appears in 3:1 — 4:13; 5:11 — 6:12; 10:19 — 12:29.

5) Dialog or interchange of speech. Many linguists do not consider dialog as a separate discourse category because — as noted above — it can be a feature of narrative or exposition. Yet it can also be classified as an independent form of discourse with its own mode of progress, namely, verbal exchange. Drama, the most characteristic form of dialog, is not found in the New Testament, but short dialogs appear.

Examples. The controversies in the Gospel of John use dialog form. Rev 7:13-17 is a dialog between the heavenly elder and the prophet. Rom 8:31-39 presents Paul's teaching on God's saving will in dialog form. Paul asks a series of rhetorical questions which he immediately answers to illustrate the certainty of salvation for those who are in Christ.

6) Performatives. These communication events fall outside of the division of discourse types according to modes of progress of the discourse. They are a special form of illocution in that they change reality by their very utterance. When a president of the United States formally nominates a person to a cabinet post, the special form of language endows the person with a new role once all legal conditions are satisfied. A judge's sentence has power in society. When

a man and a woman voice mutual fidelity in a formal marriage ceremony, their performative "I do" creates a new bond of union.

Examples. Luke 22:19-20. Jesus performs the role of creator of the Eucharist and entrusts its performance to his followers. Matt 28:18-20. As commissioned by the Father Jesus commissions his disciples as preachers and ministers of baptism.

All of these diverse forms of discourse are extended communication events. In its own way and for its own purposes, each of these is an extended exercise of the functions of speech acts isolated by Roman Jakobson and explained above in Chapter 3. This variety of discourse forms illustrates the principle of language that every element in the construction of a text in some way affects its meaning. for meaning includes everything that goes to make up a text, such as concepts, focus, emphasis, tone, word order, tense, voice. The style of an author results from an ability to combine such elements as portraying characters, highlighting a gesture, evoking receptor response, or making an argument attractive.

Examples. Luke 15:30, 32. The use of the pronoun "your" with "son" and "brother" highlight the attitudes of the merciful father and the unforgiving elder son. Mark 5:43. At the end of the account of the raising of the girl to life, Mark adds — in the style of an afterthought — that Jesus provided for her hunger. John 4:2. After recording the popular opinion that Jesus baptized, John inserts a personal denial of this fact.

THE ROLE OF LITERARY GENRES

In actual fact, every writing of the New Testament can be put into a more specific literary form or genre than the six broad categories of discourse listed above. On this level also literary critics are divided about the best way to identify and group individual literary genres. Some critics hold that the content is the essential and sufficient element for determining a form. In that case, the number of literary genres would be as large as the topics of composition, like mystery story, adventure story, romance, soap opera, character sketch, science fiction. Other critics take the exact opposite approach and identify literary genre with its formal element, the mold into which the content is poured.

Most critics, however, take a middle course and define literary genre as some special, recognizable unity of matter and form. Genres can then be understood in either the active or the passive sense. 1) In the active sense, a literary genre is the network of dynamic influences that guides both writers to shape their presentations in encoding a work and readers to formulate their expectations in decoding it. 2) In the passive sense, literary forms are a list of kinds of writings available in a literature at any given time. Thus, tablets surviving from early societies already contained mention of "oracles, hymns, incantations, codes" (Wilder: 359).

New Testament writers expressed themselves in four major literary forms: gospels, apostolic letters, acts and apocalyptic prophecy.

1) Gospel. A gospel is a structured narrative of the ministry of Jesus as a person chosen by God and tested for a unique mission. He was commissioned to reveal the Kingdom of God by word and deed. Fidelity to this mission brought Jesus into conflict with the religious leaders of his people. When he remained faithful to his mission, he was betrayed and put to death. Yet God did not abandon him but put his seal of approval on the ministry of Jesus by raising him up and sending his Holy Spirit upon his followers. The gospels are the one truly new literary genre created by the apostolic Church to provide an authoritative account of the mission of Jesus. But this literary form prevailed for only a short lifespan in orthodox Christianity. During the Patristic period it was replaced by homiletic commentaries; in modern times a great variety of lives of Jesus have appeared to supplement the gospel form.

2) Apostolic Letter. Chronologically, the first literary

form in the group of 27 writings that make up the New Testament was the authoritative letter to a group of Christians. It was created and developed by the apostle Paul. Apostolic letters are "occasional" writings, community texts sent out to direct communities who had some special need. Of course, letters existed for thousands of years before Paul wrote, but he developed a distinctive structure to serve a unique purpose in prolonging the Christ event. The form of the apostolic letter seems to be a modification of an existing letter form employed by Hellenistic philosophers. It comprises four elements:

a) salutation — a greeting to the community "in Christ," that is, a group of believers called to a life of committed faith and mutual loving concern as they supported one another in their hope that Jesus Christ would return in glory.

b) thanksgiving or liturgical telegram — outlining the topics to be developed but in the form of a thanksgiving to God. This part focused the attention of the recipients to whom the letter would be read and created a religious atmosphere for hearing its message.

c) the dialog of the letter. Usually called the "body," this consisted of both instructions for the situation and exhortations to encourage the community to rekindle its faith commitment.

d) final words — appropriate forms of greeting, often including a blessing and prayers for the recipients.

3) Acts of the Apostles. This is a unique narrative that extends the Gospel of Luke. It organizes select events from the ministry of Peter and Paul to show how the Holy Spirit guided the formation of believing communities first among Jewish disciples and then among the Gentiles until the arrival of Paul at Rome. Acts is sometimes called "the gospel of the Holy Spirit" because it provides the Church with assurance that his presence enabled believers to continue the saving work of Jesus in the world.

4) Apocalypse or Book of Revelation. This work is placed last in the collection of normative writings of the early Church. Calling itself both a revelation and a prophecy, this book offers a message of prophetic comfort to the Church in

its ambiguous position in world history. Using apocalyptic imagery that is taken chiefly from the Jewish Scriptures, its symbolic visions remind believers that the Church will always be in conflict with this world. Yet God protects his people in all trials and will bring those who remain faithful to Jesus to endless glory where they will reign with him.

The internal flow of each of these four literary genres is different. Gospels are narratives with a story line that describes the activities of Jesus and their impact on those who come into contact with him. These narratives, rich as they are in insights about Jesus, are not the only source of truth about the Christian faith. The other genres are necessary to provide the basis for the Church's worship, theology and witness.

In themselves the New Testament books do not exhaust all the possibilities of Christian theological reflection. Historically, as the Church became more complex and diversified, Christians developed other literary genres to develop their revelation. In a sense all subsequent Christian theological and spiritual writings are commentaries on Scripture, which remains the ultimate norm of faith and praxis for believers. "The fact is that there is a prior sense for the real which pervades and tests all language and all stories" (Wilder: 362).

Sources

Beekman, John; Callow, John; Kopesec, Michael, 1981, *The Semantic Structure of Written Communication.* 5th revised edition. Dallas: Summer Institute of Linguistics.

Funk, Robert W., 1966, *Language, Hermeneutic and Word of God.* NY: Harper and Row.

Louw, J. P., 1982, *Semantics of New Testament Greek.* Phila.: Fortress.

Nida, Eugene A., 1982, "A Socio-semiotic Approach to Rhetoric," Paper delivered at the Language Sciences Summer Institute, Tokyo.

Tannehill, Robert C., 1975, *The Sword of His Mouth*: *Forceful and Imaginative Language in Synoptic Sayings.* Phila.: Fortress.

Wilder, Amos N., 1983, "Story and Story-World," *Interpretation* 37: 353-364.

Chapter 7

Discourse Analysis III: Reader Response

As long as language is treated as a complete and yet open-ended sign system of communication — a form of communication that involves encoder, message and decoder — then a text is never finished. Even when the message is printed as a text, it is not the material object itself. Rather, the text remains the complex symbolic object. Since its whole purpose is to signify, it becomes text only when readers as decoders enter into dialog with it. In that dialog the text is the sign system that always produces what Charles Peirce called interpretants (described in Chapter 1). Interpretants are the ideas, conclusions and — ultimately — intellectual habits to which a sign gives rise in the minds of readers. Interpretants are themselves signs and consequently generate meaning without end. The text serves as an instrument of rhetoric, which is a feature of language that will be discussed further in the next two chapters.

Without readers as recipients, texts would not act as signs. Hence, readers play an active role in the communication events that take place. What is their role in discourse analysis? Specifically, how do readers contribute to the impact and appeal of the New Testament today? Every one of its 27 writings was composed to be read — and not merely heard by the individual addressees. The very nature of writing is to initiate communication at a distance. As an invitation to dialog, these written texts presumed that their readers had the experience of other texts (Eco: 21). The authors assumed that their readers could integrate their writings into an ongoing communication process.

Wolfgang Iser describes the relation between author and reader in terms of two poles: as creator, the author is the artistic pole and the readers, who effect any realization of the text, are the aesthetic pole. If readers fail to bring spiritual openness and commitment to their reading of the New Testament, they prevent its message from transforming their lives.

Examples. Mark 7:19. This short comment on the action of Jesus as "purifying all food" invites readers to participate in the power of his action. Mark 13:14. The author inserts a note within the discourse to alert readers to these warnings. In 1 Cor 3:1 Paul refers to a lack of spiritual discernment that is hindering the Corinthians from being ready to hear the good news of salvation.

An examination of the history of interpretation of passages from the New Testament makes it clear that commentators in the different historical periods of the Church saw different meanings in the same text. From Patristic times they understood passages as addressing problems of their own age or applied them to situations for which they were searching answers. This traditional method of decoding the New Testament indicates that believers always considered its writings as having multi-level meanings: they embody multiplex features that operate simultaneously on more than one level of reality. For example, as discourse the text communicates not only on the level of individual words (which can be extracted and expanded into theological themes), but also on the level of individual sentences or propositions (which can serve as rallying cries for religious response), and finally as a complete literary creation (which contains an integrated message within the total canon of Scripture).

Medieval scholastic commentators further developed the Patristic theory of the fourfold meaning of Scripture: the literal, moral, allegorical and anagogic or eschatological senses. This framework served as an instrument to extract the theological richness of its message. Modern literary critics like Susan Wittig express appreciation for this insight but prefer to use terms like multiple or polyvalent or multi-level meaning and to speak of the plurisignificance of a text. What they stress is that this semantic diversity is not imposed upon the text from outside by readers but belongs to the very form of the text. That is why Wittig recommends Peirce's semiotic model as a way of coming to understand the full range of meaning in New Testament writings. "It can help to establish not only a way of understanding how meaning is achieved but a model for organizing ways of understanding meaning" (Wittig: 78).

Because readers come to a text from different directions than the author, they fill in the blanks — which every text necessarily contains — from their own background and experience, that is, "from a personal ideological perspective" (Eco: 22). This diversity generates their creative contribution to discourse analysis. In entering into this dialog readers are not acting in a purely arbitrary manner but are constrained by indications contained in the text itself.

Example. In 2 Thess 2:5, the readers are asked to remember what Paul had told them while he was with them. They receive a warning not to go beyond proper limits in interpreting the tradition about the return of Jesus. In the conflict about how to understand that return, they must bring their belief into conformity with the revelation preached to them by Paul.

As mentioned in speaking of implicature in Chapter 4, readers as decoders of a message must bring their resources to bear to integrate its many linguistic features. Only in this way can they hear the semantic kernels that support the surface structure. By that process they understand why the author chose this kind of surface structure. Readers also become aware of nonlinguistic elements of the author's situation that cling to the text. These are social and personal forces that continuously color the author's choice of material and mode of expression. In addition to general cultural influences, nonlinguistic elements include the whole range of subconscious and nonconsious dimensions that the behavioral sciences investigate as well as human emotions.

Example. 1 Thess 2:14-16. Paul introduces abruptly a polemic against the Jews. Logically, it does not fit but it may reflect Paul's hurt at the harassment he has received from them.

All these qualities of language employed by an author to make the text aesthetically attractive and to evoke emotions in the audience belong under the heading of rhetorical features or literary style. Readers must be sensitive to them to experience the full impact of the text. Nonconceptual elements make up an integral part of the message of a text, which is a unity produced by the marriage of matter and form. Poetic texts tend to be richer in the figurative use of language and usually contain many figures of speech, like balance, metaphor, irony, artistic arrangements and hyperbole or exaggeration. Such figures are chiefly responsible for the appeal a text has and the impact it creates. They focus attention on the connotations of the text rather than on its denotative or conceptual meaning. They embody a suggestiveness that invites us as readers "to adapt our personal world to the emotional world possessed by the text" (Eco: 53).

In this context it is clear that every narrative is written from some perspective, technically called its "point of view," which includes both expression and content. "Point of view" admits of wide variation and degrees of sophistication that have been studied only to a limited extent thus far, but which have important bearing on the total impact of texts. Even a simple and straightforward religious narrative signifies abiding human values that invite readers to respond by involving them in the story. Seldom do narrators say specifically that they are communicating second-level significance, but the way they unfold events reveals abiding values for their readers.

Three qualities that enable readers to carry out their active role in helping the text to its goal are:

1) Imagination. Imagination enables readers to probe the text by as many methods as possible until they understand its message thoroughly and celebrate its significance in a variety of responses. Part II will discuss imagination at length.

Example. Matt 13:43, "He who has ears, let him hear!" — a phrase that occurs often in the New Testament — invites reader response so that the text will reveal its impact and challenges.

2) Retrospection. A religious text asks readers to examine their personal consciousness, memory and experience in a new light in order to enter into its message totally. "Apply yourself wholly to the text; apply the text wholly to you."

Example. 2 Peter 3:14-16 speaks of qualities that believers need to correspond to the demands of Scripture.

3) Responsibility, in the religious sense of giving priority to God's message. All religious language is God-ward. Every encounter with the New Testament demands decision: it draws readers toward committing themselves to God's will or becomes the occasion of turning away from it.

Over and above these three qualities, as human language changes with social conditions, readers find it harder to comprehend and relate to those many features of the New Testament that grew out of a culture much different from that of today. In fact, commentaries are needed to provide background so that modern readers can hear the text clearly and without disrupting static. The accomplishments of human progress including greater psychological awareness often create expectations different from those who first heard the New Testament writings. False expectations distort the message and block fruitful reader exchange with it.

Because of a unique set of experiences, each reader hears

and interacts with the text in a uniquely personal way. This does not imply that interpretation is a purely subjective and individualistic activity. The New Testament is the sacred and normative library of the Christian community. As such, it is best read in a community setting and in the light of tradition. Mutual reflection and prayerful sharing of the text stimulates individual members in hearing and responding to the message.

Example. Col 4:16. Paul tells the community to exchange this letter with the community of Laodicea and to read his letter to them.

Among all the passages in the New Testament perhaps the parables are the ones that are presented in the way that best enfolds readers in the dialog of personal surrender to God's transcendent will as expressed in a plan which is often called salvation history. The suggested applications that follow some gospel parables serve as models finding other meanings inherent in them and as invitations to prolong the interpretative process. Only in this exchange does the parable become a communication event and an ongoing source of creative dialog for readers.

Examples. Mark 4:3-9 + 14-20. The Parable of the Sower with the interpretation of it from tradition as the Parable of the Seed is put first in the parable discourse found in all three Synoptic Gospels. This interpretation suggests that it was a parable about how to hear parables. It illustrates the power of parables to divide their audience into those who accept the working of God's grace in their lives and those who harden themselves against his word. 2 Peter 1:20-21 posits the need of a special help to understand the prophetic words. The Holy Spirit, who originally inspired the prophets, must also empower readers to understanding their message.

The link between interpretation and the divine help called inspiration will be treated in Chapters 20-21. The necessarily active part that readers must take in appropriating the message of the New Testament raises a variety of questions about the nature of biblical inspiration that will be dealt with there.

Modern studies on "the role of the reader" and "the implied reader" and "reader-response criticism" investigate questions about how a text is "open" and capable of stimulating behavioral responses among readers. This area of research is of special interest for religious texts. This reader openness does not mean that a text has no boundaries or remains ultimately ambiguous. In creating a text as a complex symbol formed by carefully blending language resources, an author guides readers along carefully constructed trajectories to truth and value.

Example. Gal 4:21-27. Paul reads the remarks in the Book of Genesis about Abraham as an allegory of the two covenants between God and his people and uses it as an invitation to believe.

At times the gaps to be filled in by modern readers of the New Testament, especially Paul's letters, present stiff challenges. Even professional commentators differ about the best way to approach many parts of the text.

Examples. 1 Cor 7 — 15. Paul's way of presenting this material shows that he is responding to specific questions addressed to him by a divided community; different groups took contradictory approaches. He is sensitive to a variety of opinions that mean little to modern readers. In 1 Cor 4:19 Paul recognizes that this letter is not going to settle all of their difficulties and expresses his hope to come again to assert his authority to eliminate the divisions among them.

Another aspect of reader response to New Testament texts is to determine the tone of individual passages. At times writers display strong feelings or engage in polemics or employ figures of speech to achieve a desired effect. More will be said about such artistic use of language in the next two chapters.

Example. Heb 12:4-13. This text appeals to readers by contrasting their timidity with the courageous "cloud of witnesses" down through Israel's history. They remained loyal to God in the face of obstacles.

Sources

Boucher, Madeleine I., 1981, *The Parables.* Wilmington: Michael Glazier.

Eco, Umberto, 1979, *The Role of the Reader.* Bloomington: Indiana U. Press.

Iser, Wolfgang, 1974, *The Implied Reader.* Baltimore: Johns Hopkins U. Press.

Tompkins, Jane P., ed., 1980, *Reader-Response Criticism: From Formalism to Post-Structuralism.* Baltimore: Johns Hopkins U. Press.

Wittig, Susan, 1977, "A Theory of Multiple Meanings," *Semeia* 9:75-101.

Chapter 8

Artistry in Language Communication

For almost 2,000 years the New Testament has played the role of a classic, a religious masterpiece. It has exercised power over society as a whole as well as over individual readers. Besides functioning as an organ of communication, it has also evoked response by the aesthetic beauty of its discourse. Why does it have power to move readers? How does it enlighten and influence them? Where does it get its continual appeal and impact — the marks of literary excellence?

The quality that makes a literary work pleasing is called style, which is the result of a mastery of the art of rhetoric. Rhetoric is operative at two levels: the general or macro-and the particular or micro-, as Eugene Nida explained (see Chapter 6). Macrorhetoric operates on the level of discourse as a structured work with unity, coherence and prominence. It will be studied in this chapter. Microrhetoric, which is seen most clearly in the use of figures of speech, will be treated in the next chapter.

One of the six functions of a speech act or communication event in the schema of Roman Jakobson (studied in Chapter 3) is the "poetic." The poetic is the function a text enjoys as a literary artifact, as an artistic blend of matter and form created to delight readers. One of the attractive features of poetic style is the skillful choosing of vocabulary to give the text rhythm or melodious tone. In straightforward prose an author selects from vocabulary available in the language those terms that achieve a desired meaning effect with proper contrast, appeal, direction, insight and urgency. But when authors wish to concentrate on the text itself, they give primary attention to considerations of sound — like the kind of vowels and the length and number of syllables — in combining words. The result is a text with a density of texture that engages readers more intensely. Consider the power of Poe's "Quoth the Raven, 'Nevermore.'"

It should be noted, however, that to have a "poetic" function, a text does not have to be composed in verse form, with a fixed kind of regularity. Rather, the essential feature of the poetic function is a close correlation between structure and meaning. "Poeticity is present when the word is felt as a word...when words and their composition, their meaning, their external and inner form acquire a weight and a value of their own instead of referring indifferently to reality" (Jakobson, 1981: 750). Ordinarily a text that is written with rhetorical flourish will contain more figurative or second-level language, and thus make more demands on readers for their participation.

Example. Col 1:15-20 is a hymn to the so-called cosmic Christ. It has qualities of poetic language without being written in a regular rhythm.

George Lakoff and Mark Johnson have proposed that metaphor is central to all language because the prevailing system of conceptualizing is fundamentally metaphorical in nature. Their theory could explain why artistic speech builds so much on images. At the same time, image thinking needs to be developed by individuals and incorporated into the system of meaningful sounds that makes up a language.

Only then can images be communicated and shared by generating new images.

The experiences, images, values, hopes, fears, goals, ideas and ideals of early Christian communities were expressed in a variety of imaginative styles, as is witnessed by the writings preserved in the New Testament. This traditional collection makes these experiences available for the instruction, comfort and celebration of each successive generation of Christian believers, who must be introduced into the language and practices of their ancestors in the faith.

The verbal signs of the New Testament no longer ring out loud and clear to contemporary Christians because of the major changes in language, culture and self-consciousness that have taken place in the world since that time. As a result, specialists and commentators are needed to recover the artistry of early Christian rhetoric, to freshen images dulled by use, to revitalize stale metaphors, and to perform all the translation tasks involved in making the original religious experience once more accessible in all its wonder and saving power. Only then will the New Testament become once more the true "universe of discourse" for the Christian community, a comprehensive, structured world that can be shared and celebrated joyfully (see Jakobson: 1976).

This translation task goes far beyond the transfer of information. it means encoding the original signs of revelation into what Amos Wilder calls a "theopoetic" (see Chapter 19), that is, a voice that speaks to the needs of contemporaries in the images of our time. If successful, this translation will have an expressive and emotive power comparable to the poetic power of the original message. The resulting synthesis will enable readers to "feel" the power of the original as the new voice experienced by participants of the Christ event. This does not mean that the exterior form or surface structure will look exactly the same as the original. Part II will deal with the role of imagination in this translation.

The particular macrorhetorical features that appear in the New Testament depend upon the literary genres employed; these were explained in Chapter 6. Narratives have a different style, perspective, pace and movement than letters; only narratives are divided into episodes. The snatches of verse embedded in the different books are more compact in form than the hortatory passages — and so on. The referential meaning of the various New Testament books can be translated exactly with relative ease into modern languages, despite the fact that their concepts may now seem dull because of frequent repetition and commentary.

The artistry of these writings is linked more directly to their emotive meanings, which are "essentially analogical, and must be explained in terms of degrees of reaction." As Eugene Nida goes on to elaborate, "Emotive meanings are describable, not in terms of bundles of distinctive conceptual features, but in terms of types and degrees of emotional reaction to the expressions of language" (Nida, 1975: 18). Their focus is *parole* or speech, the manner in which structure manifests itself in actual discourse. This dimension of style is often lost in translation.

Style always embraces at least two levels of meaning: besides denotation it includes allusions and all other kinds of interaction with the cultural setting. Such allusions in the New Testament are lost for unprepared contemporary readers. These dynamic factors are too closely linked to its original setting to be immediately available to modern cultural patterns. "Form A conveys one meaning experience, form B another, and this difference is what style is about," for "a critical awareness of style (is) the capacity to respond perceptively to linguistic variation" (Wendland: 118).

Three qualities are essential for achieving good style: a) discernment — a capacity to make correct judgments about what is appropriate for the text in terms of vocabulary, level of discourse, linguistic and nonlinguistic circumstances; b) choice — the ability to pick formal elements that will convey this critical judgment and give proper tone to the work. In that sense, "meaning is choice," because there is no distinctive and personal contribution without an author's ability to make choices of style; c) creativity — that elusive gift of combining linguistic elements in a new mix that sparkles with color and verve.

These qualities of style do not function in a vacuum but are linked to the content of a literary work in such a way as to achieve the necessary unity, coherence and prominence required of a great text. Historically, writings that deal with religion have acquired a recognizable "religious style and vocabulary." These flow ultimately from the "primary religious experience" that was originally expressed in the myth or foundation event — "in the sense of highly figurative language employed to explain the ultimate reality of cosmological and supernatural events and values" (Nida, 1981: 111). Original attempts to portray God and his intervention with respect to human destiny exhibit a large component of figurative language because such primary religious experience was so personal and emotionally overpowering. Later the experience was put into abstract language and codified in systematic treatises of theology.

Example. The author of the letter to the Hebrews shows a masterful expository style. He announces a thesis and then unfolds this announcement by using imagery from the great Jewish feast of Atonement (Yom Kippur) to show how the death of Jesus is sacrificial. He involves his readers by alternately using instruction and exhortation. In Chapter 11 he includes a pose hymn or aretalogy to the heroes of faith — a hymn marked by the striking use of assonance in the repetition of the word "faith."

All writings of the New Testament have characteristics of primary religious language, although some, like Hebrews, are moving toward systematic formulation. All belong to the area of axiology in that they stress value and responsibility and foster the synthetic imagination. that dimension of the New Testament will be studied in Part II of this work.

Sources

Jakobson, Roman, 1976, "A Few Remarks on Structuralism," *Modern Language Notes* 91:1534-1539.

_____1981, "What is Poetry?" *Selected Writings.* The Hague: Mouton, 3: 740-750.

Lakoff, George and Johnson, Mark, 1980, *Metaphors We Live By.* Chicago: U. of Chicago Press.

Nida, Eugene A., 1975, Exploring Semantic Structures. Munchen: Wilhelm Fink Verlag.

_____1981, *Sign, Sense, Translation.* Pretoria: U. of Pretoria

Wendland, Ernest R., 1972 "Receptor Language Style and Bible Translation, III: Training Translators about Style," *The Bible Translator* 33: 115-127.

Chapter 9

Figures of Speech and Language

Style is not an ornament added to meaning but a personal dimension of it. In addition to the macrorhetoric treated in the last chapter, style takes the form of specific figures of speech that can be analyzed and classified. The fact that it is possible to classify figures of speech shows that they are not entirely spontaneous but have become a predictable part of discourse. Hence, linguists distinguish between figurative language, which is still creative and unforeseen, and figures of speech, which are a conventional way of stretching language into new forms of meaning.

Example. Luke 13:1 speaks of Pilate as mixing the blood of pilgrims with their sacrifices. This is a figurative use of language to describe their death in a vivid image.

Because figurative language reflects the culture in which it springs up, it may not be appealing in another culture. At the same time, figurative speech as such is a language universal and "in varying degrees figurative expressions are used to express many types of experience, especially psychological attitudes and expressions" (Nida and Reyburn: 41). Because skill in analyzing emotive dimensions of language has not matched advances in logical analysis, descriptions of figurative language are not as specific and exact as terms for designating denotative forms. What figurative language lacks in clarity, however, it more than supplies in impact and appeal.

One of the characteristics of figurative language, if not its distinguishing mark, is that it is harder to understand for non-native speakers, that is, for those outside of the culture from which it springs. Frequently it cannot be translated directly into other languages. For example, the characteristic of Hebrew poetic style, namely, parallelism (repeating the idea or image in a similar way in the second half of a verse) is not a feature of English verse, which is marked by extremely concentrated expression and provocative combinations of words. The Hebrew prophets gave their oracles against Israel in verse, contrary to the style of contemporary prophetic witness. Much of what is referred to in New Testament commentaries as poetry does not read like poetry in English. Creative rendering of biblical figurative language demands the use of other kinds of figures and images to capture the original connotations.

Example. John 1:1-5 + 9-12 is written in Hebrew verse style, that is, in parallel lines, but English readers can scarcely comprehend it as poetic. In fact, other more subtle forms of parallelism exist that give texts a richness that untrained modern readers do not suspect.

On the whole, the New Testament does not contain as much figurative language as classical Greek texts, but it does have sufficient figures of speech for them to be treated in this chapter. Moreover, there is a figurative dimension of its language that does not appear in English translations because it is related to Greek syntax, which is much different than English. For example, Greek style includes artistic variation in word order (hyperbaton). That type of variation is practically impossible to reproduce in English. Such figures will not be treated here. This chapter will deal only with figures of speech and figures of language that have comparable forms in English.

A. Figures of speech significant for interpreting the New Testament are:

1) Metaphor — an implied comparison by the stretching of words beyond literal usage.

Example. 1 Tim 1:19 speaks of some members of the community as being "shipwrecked on their faith."

Metaphors are extremely important in New Testament writings chiefly because the most distinctive form of preaching of Jesus was the parable, which is an extended metaphor. In recent years parables have received a lion's share of attention in gospel study. In 1974 the first two volumes of the experimental biblical journal *Semeia* were devoted to parables, and whole university courses investigate them. How parables convey meaning is still disputed, but an effective approach is to divide them into "vehicle" and "tenor." The vehicle is the exterior, the image or medium that opens up readers to the tenor or new way of seeing the subject of the metaphor. Aristotle held that to be "master of the metaphor" was the greatest sign of genius, an ability that was inborn and unteachable (*Rhetoric* 1459a). Metaphors can cease to be living and yet still remain stock metaphors. These "have an important social function in expressing and reinforcing the accepted system of order or belief" (Caird: 153).

Frequently throughout Christian history commentators stressed or created allegorical dimensions of New Testament parables. This process began in the gospels themselves. For example, Mark offers an allegorical interpretation of the parable of the sower by explaining the various types of seeds as ways of reacting to the word of God (Mark 4:14-20). Not all parables are allegories, which is a second-level interpretation of the elements in the parable according to some principle of religious insight. The key to many allegorical parables is the concept of the Kingdom of God.

Example. Matt 13:36-43 is an allegorical interpretation of

the parable of the weeds, in terms of the last judgment that passes on entrance to the Kingdom.

Umberto Eco sees the possibility of metaphor as rooted in the "multidimensional network of metonymies," that is, of those words that can be substituted for one another (Eco: 74). Language divides reality into a series of arbitrary contiguities that reflect cultural values. That is, words are "territories of meaning" that are divided by arbitrary convention in different languages. These semiotic links are imaginatively extended by the artistic stretching of language. Perhaps the most important consideration for understanding how parables function is to recognize that they depend not upon the denotative or primarily conceptual elements of words but upon some connotative element. Unless the reader is able to recognize the underlying connotation, the metaphor will not reveal the intended meaning but will actually mislead.

Example. In John's Gospel, Jesus continually addresses God as "father." This metaphor is based not on the literal sense of a father as physical procreator, but upon certain connotative dimensions of the father image in the ancient Near East, that is, a father as protector, provider, educator, support.

In New Testament studies the term metaphor covers also the figure of speech called "simile," in which the comparison is explicit.

Example. Rev 3:3. I come "like a thief," that is, unexpectedly — an image to focus on the swiftness and unpredictable element in divine judgment.

2) Hyperbole, or exaggeration, and its opposite, litotes or understatement, serve as figures to heighten the impact of a statement. Note that emphasis is achieved by either figure, much in the same way as a speaker can emphasize a point by raising or lowering volume.

Examples. Matt 4:8. The picture of the temptation is deliberately exaggerated, that is, no mountain can be so high that

Jesus could have seen all the world's glory. Rom 1:16, "I am not ashamed of the gospel" is Paul's low keyed way of affirming his total trust in the revelation of Jesus as unique message of God's salvation.

3) Personification. This occurs when an author treats an animal or some object as if it were endowed with human properties.

Example. James 3:5-6. James treats the tongue as if it were a ruler, reigning over the human person and causing all kinds of evil by its immoral conduct.

4) Apostrophe — often linked to personification — is directly addressing either the readers or a character in the text or some situation. It is a rhetorical device for an author to express in tense emotion or to emphasize a point.

Example. Gal 3:1. Paul speaks directly to his readers, "O foolish Galatians," to dramatize his hurt.

B. Noteworthy figures of language in the New Testament, that is, artistic modes of communication, include:

1) Artistic word patters. This heading embraces various kinds of repetition that give a passage special literary power:

a) anaphora or repetition of a key word at the beginning of successive phrases or sentences.

Example. Matt 23:13, 14, 15, 16, 23, 25, 27, 29, "Woe to you!" The anaphora at the beginning of each lament in this series of anti-beatitudes communicates a sense of the imminent conflict about to erupt between Jesus and his opponents.

b) inclusion, that is, the repetition of a key expression at beginning and end of a passage in order to set it off as a unity. Inclusion makes for a sandwich effect.

Examples. James 2:20-26. In this paragraph about faith without works being useless, even dead, the phrase "faith without works" at beginning and end forms an inclusion. On a grander scale Matthew links 1:23 and 28:20 by a subtle inclusion. He interprets the name given to the child, Emmanuel, as "God with us." The final words of Jesus as he takes leave of his disciples refers to this name by promising, "I am with you all days."

c) flashbacks — repetition of key words or phrases later in the work to reinforce the impact.

Example. Matt 16:6-12. Jesus uses references to his two miracles of multiplying bread to contrast his nourishing teaching to the corrupt teaching of the Pharisees.

The use of language patterns can extend beyond individual words to the arranging of scenes.

Example. John 13:31-14:31. The exchanges between Jesus and his disciples are arranged in an artistic "revelation pattern," which consists of three elements: a revelation by Jesus, a question by a disciple, and a clarification by Jesus (see below in Chapter 22). John uses this pattern in several places to portray Jesus as acting simultaneously on two levels: the visible or passing and the mysterious or abiding levels of reality.

2) Rhetorical questions. These are a special kind of question placed in a text not to gather information but to serve a stylistic function, for example, to arouse attention, to express surprise, to provide focus, or to change the flow of discourse. Katherine Barnwell states that about 700 of the approximately 1,000 questions in the New Testament are rhetorical (Barnwell: 90). Paul is fond of this technique to increase the dynamic impact of his advice. Among the evangelists Luke, who shows great sensitivity to style, often employs rhetorical questions.

Example. Luke 16:3. The manager expresses his dilemma in a rhetorical question.

3) Irony — expressing meaning by saying the opposite of what is known or felt. Irony must be recognized from the context, which indicates to readers that a figure of language is involved. It is often joined to sarcasm. The irony of the

New Testament is traditional or polemic irony, not the so-called "romantic irony" of paradoxical style.

Example. 1 Cor 1:4-8. Paul speaks ironically in this opening thanksgiving because the letter will reveal that the Corinthians are not actually "rich in everything."

Like idioms, figures of speech and language are often tied to aspects of a particular culture. Hence, they may not be evident in an English translation because translators have modified the form of expression. They form part of the connotative dimension of texts that is difficult to deal with in translation. This dimension of meaning is also part of reality, however, and the next chapter will reflect upon it.

Sources

Barnwell, Kathleen, 1980, *Introduction to Semantics and Translation.* Second ed. Horsleys Green, England: Summer Institute of Linguistics.

Caird, G. B., 1980, *The Language and Images of the Bible.* Phila.: Westminster Press.

Eco, Umberto, 1979, "The Semantics of Metaphor," Chapter 3 of *The Role of the Reader.* Bloomington: Indiana U. Press.

Nida, Eugene A., 1982, "A Semantic Approach to Rhetoric," Paper delivered at the Language Sciences Summer Institute, Tokyo.

Nida, Eugene A. and Reyburn, William D., 1981, *Meaning Across Cultures.* Maryknoll, NY: Orbis Books.

Patte, Daniel, 1979, "From Narrative Analysis to Semiotic Theory: Syntagmatic and Paradigmatic," Paper privately printed. Nashville: Vanderbilt U.

Chapter 10

Meaning and Reality

What is meaning? How does it relate to language? How are they the same? These and similar questions surface as we try to analyze what happens when we study the New Testament as a classical text of the world's religious traditions, and specifically as the normative canon of all Christian churches.

Before looking at how language means, it is important to state that language is not the only meaning system. Semiotics, or the study of signs, protects us from reducing all reality to language, which is only one of several sign systems employed by humans. Language is unique in that it is limited to humans (technically, it is a species-specific system), but humans have other sign systems in common with brute animals (Deely: 116). Humans share sense experience and perception with other animals but, thanks to language, they are able to share among themselves "post linguistic structures" like civil government and religious traditions, in a word, a whole "cultural system" (107-123). Language then is an essential part of human reality but not its totality. As the sign system that is unique to humans, it provides them with a method of communication that commands special concern and investigation.

Any form of division of reality is artificial and rests on presuppositions. For example, structuralism uses the technique of binary opposition. But a more fruitful approach for drawing out the implications of written discourse is the threefold method of Charles Peirce, already mentioned in Chapter 1, namely: 1) firstness or immediacy — the first impression arising from contact on the level of sensation or perception or even initial intellectual awareness; 2) secondness, or the act of specific analysis of an event or object in its concrete relationships to unpack this situation in itself, its structure, its inner dynamism; 3) thirdness, or the locating of this immediate knowledge, experience or relationship within the context of reality, in its interrelationships with other objects of knowledge as regards its implications for reality as a whole.

Looked at as a sign system, language offers these three dimensions in open-ended, flexible and constantly adapting signs. That is its strength. But these resources can also be used to deceive, mislead, confuse, obscure or bully into compliance or complacency. Language does not automatically usher its users into reality. No language "is perfectly consistent with itself," nor is it a "closed system" that can be mastered (Ong: 169).

Given the vast range of language and its implications, the danger is that we become overwhelmed by the complex terminology rather than develop an integrated understanding. Before proceeding to the next chapter to look at the ways historical criticism has developed to interpret the New Testament, I want to first explain briefly the kinds of meaning that can be found in it. The analysis of the communication event according to the schema of Roman Jakobson (see Chapter 3) warns against contracting the meaning of meaning in any way. Meaning is an analogous term. With respect to a written text, it applies to both the comprehensive study of understanding as a whole as well as to the various levels of understanding involved in its components: from the usage of individual words, to sentences, to the role and thrust of sections, to the work as a whole.

As Eugene Nida explained, when applied to a word in a

text, meaning is "a set of relations for which a verbal symbol is a sign" (Nida, 1975b: 14). On an existential level, meaning embraces the choices that readers make as a result of encountering the text to make it "meaningful" to them (Nida, 1981: 40). Meaning also refers to the intention of the New Testament writers who communicated a set of choices and values to the apostolic communities. Common belief in the resurrection of the earthly Jesus brought new identity to those who accepted him as their risen Lord. They in turn created out of their new experiences a different world, a "new creation" (Gal 6:15). For them it was a new common identity giving the power that originated in faith, found expression in mutual love and enjoyed the transcendent hope of sharing in the lordship of Jesus forever.

This library of religious writings formed the universe of discourse for communities of Christians who came together to celebrate their common hope. Only after the Enlightenment did these writings become the object of critical scrutiny as part of the critical scene of the eighteenth century, when authors started to address mass audiences. With the rise of literary criticism the various types of meaning found in the New Testament came to be analyzed. Following Nida, we can treat them under two principal headings: referential and associated.

1. *Referential Meaning.* Strictly speaking, as was explained in Chapter 2, words in themselves as signs do not "have" meaning as if it were an object, but rather are nuclei of "meaning potential." Each verbal sign has parameters of that potential. The realities to which individual words may refer are called their referential meaning. This territory is better discovered by the experience of usage in a speech community than by looking up the word in a dictionary.

The dimensions of possible meaning can be analyzed by a process known as componential analysis. This is a process of dividing reality systematically at every level of comprehension into the possible semantic domains, categories and classes. Nida states the basis of this approach when he writes, "A meaning is not a thing in itself, but only a set of contrastive relations" (Nida, 1975a: 151). The goal of componential analysis is to isolate the semantic features and markers of words on various levels. The four most universal semantic domains, which Nida calls their deep-structure semotatic classes, are: objects or things, events or states, abstracts, relations (see Chapter 2). Within these universal domains an indefinite number of smaller semantic categories are evident, for example, colors, kinds of animals, means of human communication.

Each language makes its own classifications of these semantic domains, and they are never the same in any two languages. Ordinarily the divisions are not scientific but rather reflect popular outlook and culture. For several years Nida has been working on a dictionary for New Testament translators in which its total vocabulary will be organized according to semantic categories and word fields. This will enable translators to see clearly how words in the same fields are employed and thus how they interrelate. The 5,000 plus terms of the New Testament have more than 20,000 meanings, because the same word often has meanings in more than one word field. Such usage illustrates Nida's observation that "the referent of a verbal symbol is not an object in the practical world; rather it is a concept or set of concepts which people may have about objects, events, abstracts and relations" (Nida, 1975b: 14).

Many problems arise in trying to place terms in their proper referential categories, such as: a) a lack of adequate referential terms in a language to describe all the components of meaning, or in more technical terminology, the appropriate metalanguage to identify these components; b) the amazing complexity of creation that requires too many components to identify exactly all existing creatures, such as the millions of hues and shades that the human eye can distinguish or the millions of insects that exist; c) a lack of direct connection between the referential components of words and their grammatical usage, that is, the frequent skewing between semantic or deep structure meaning and the surface or grammatical usage. Thus, abstracts may appear in English as nouns or verbs.

Example. Some events in the New Testament have the grammatical form of nouns rather than verbs. In Eph 1:7 "the blood of Christ" means the event of his dying as a voluntary self-offering for sin. In 1 Cor 13 "love" is the better "way" of living.

The study of the referential meaning of the vocabulary of the New Testament offers important insights for understanding the Christian message about the human condition.

Example. The so-called "vice lists" give an insight into the Christian moral ideal; see 1 Tim 6:4-5; 2 Tim 3:2-5; Gal 5:20-21; Eph 4:31. Obviously contrasting qualities are to be nourished; see Phil 4:8; Gal 5:22-23; Eph 4:32.

The two most common procedures for componential analysis of referents are:

a) hierarchical, that is, fitting words on various levels according to the extension of the referents by means of their individual features.

Example. 1 Tim 3:1 — 5:25 deals with levels of authority that existed in the local community, although the interrelationships are no longer clear on some points.

b) Horizontal, that is showing relationships between terms that overlap or are complementary or contiguous.

Example. Eph 5:22 — 6:9. This passage speaks of members of the extended household and their mutual responsibilities: wives and husbands; children and fathers; slaves and masters.

Componential analysis is easiest for names of objects, which can often be put into the hierarchical order of increasing specificity. It becomes more difficult when applied to the relating of activities, which usually overlap. Componential analysis may also be applied to relationships, for example: time (like, before, after, simultaneous); cause and effect; conditions; logical links.

Example. Mark 1:15. "Repent" may be analyzed into three states: implied state, that the person was a sinner; transitional state of rejecting this past; resulting state of adopting a new form of life in accord with God's will.

The schemas produced by componential analysis are never completely satisfying because the semantic space within any language is never orderly, static or completely logical, but is always in the process of change. No language contains any two words that are exactly synonymous, but many are close enough to be substituted for others in some contexts so that, for example, they can be used to avoid repetition or to vary style. Also, holes exist in classification because no language provides all the metalanguage necessary to describe every possible "contrastive relation." In addition, no semantic analysis is purely objective because each person's linguistic experience is unique. Within each language group experiences are close enough to make communication possible but never completely perfect.

2. *Associated Meanings of Words.* Eugene Nida estimates that the informative function accounts for less than 5% of all communication (Nida, 1981: 25). This is true for the New Testament, which often supposes awareness in readers about situations in the community. These other kinds of meaning, designated by the term "associated meanings," can be dealt with briefly here because they correlate well with the six functions of communication event listed in Chapter 3. They are:

a) connotative meaning — the culturally conditioned emotional responses evoked by particular words. The connotation may be favorable or unfavorable, and it may be modified as changes take place in a language over a period of time.

Examples. Luke 18:9. The term Pharisee here connotes those who "trust in themselves and despise others." This meaning arose out of historical associations of Christian communities rather than denoting the actual mentality of this class of Jews at the time of Jesus. Mark 7:27. The Jewish custom of calling pagans "dogs" has the connotation of contempt. In 1 John 2:12-14 the titles "children, fathers,

young men, infants" connote various feelings toward segments of the community.

   b) reflected meaning — overtones that words convey
because of associations they reflect.

Example. Mark 1:6. The food and clothing of John the
Baptizer reflected the custom of the conservative prophetic
group.

   c) stylistic meaning — the tone that makes certain words
appropriate for a particular social usage.

Example. 1 Peter 1:3-4 imitates the bureaucratic style of the
contemporary inscriptions erected to honor public
benefactors.

   d) idiomatic meaning — the meaning that certain fixed
phrases have as a whole. it does not correspond to the literal
meaning of the individual words involved.

Example. Phil 2:12 (and several other times in the New
Testament). The phrase "with fear and trembling" does not
designate psychological fear but rather a form of profound
respect that is closer to the English phrase "with religious
awe."

   e) grammatical meaning — the meaning that results from
the lexical form that is used to call attention to a particular
circumstance. A small phonetic change, like the vowel that
puts a word into another mood or tense or case, can have a
strong impact on the meaning of a phrase.

Examples. John 20:31. In stating the purpose of this gospel,
the manuscripts are divided between the grammatical forms
pisteuēte, "that you keep believing," implying that it is for
those who are already believers, and *pisteusēte*, "that you
may come to believe," implying that it is addressed to those
not yet baptized to draw them to faith. In Col 1:16, the term
describing Christ's role in a simple past tense — that everything "was created" in Christ — appears a second time in the
more emphatic perfect tense — that everything "is fixed in
its created state" through and in Christ.

f) figurative extensions of meaning — namely, the figures of speech discussed in Chapter 7. In terms, of meaning, figurative language opens up possibilities of discovering further depths of reality as it presses on and extends the limits of language.

Example. 1 Cor 6:15. Paul sees believers as "members of Christ," an insight that expands in further references to the church as the "Body of Christ" in 1 Cor, 2 Cor, Rom, Col, Eph. This figurative stretching of language is characteristic of religious language, which communicates the new experiences of early believers.

All of these lexical units are the signs out of which discourses are formed. When studied from a semiotic perspective, that is, in terms of language as a sign system, the discourse of the New Testament is the normative part of a complex, ongoing, expanding "universe of discourse" centering around the Christ event, the most real world of early believers. For modern readers the process of finding meaning in these texts involves a series of probes or guesses or bets about the individual communication events and about the books as a whole until the construction of a personal synthesis of all their elements is achieved by discovering their unity, coherence and prominence.

The historical dimension must necessarily be incorporated into this search for the meaning of the New Testament because meaning is always linked to culture, both the culture of the time when these writings were written and the time when they are being read. That does not mean that the philogical history of each individual word must be known, because in a text the meaning comes from the context rather than from the etymology of the words.

Example. John 21:15-17. Jesus asks Peter if he "loves" him three times. In the Greek text Jesus uses the verb *agapaō* in the first two questions but *phileō* in the third. In all three cases Peter answers with the verb *phileō*. Hence, these two verbs are here used without any difference in meaning; the variation is purely stylistic (Nida 1981: 61-63).

In some instances language encompasses large segments of reality under a single verbal symbol. Millions of hues and shades are grouped under the single term "green," and the extent of the territory of meaning of such a word will vary from language to language. The findings of depth psychology indicate that words have implications that have not yet been recognized or studied. Walter Ong relates that psycholinguistic area of language to the oral nature of a mother tongue, in contrast to the effect of a learned language (Ong:163). These are questions that go beyond the scope of this introduction and await further research.

Sources

Deely, John, 1982, *Introducing Semiotic: Its History and Doctrine.* Bloomington: Indiana U. Press.

Nida, Eugene A., 1975a, "Techniques for Analyzing Single Referential Meaning," *Componential Analysis of Meaning.* The Hague: Mouton, 151-173.

_____ 1975b, *Exploring Semantic Structures.* Munchen: Wilhelm Fink Verlag.

_____ 1981, *Signs, Sense, Translation.* Pretoria: University of Pretoria.

Ong, Walter J., 1982, *Orality and Literacy; The Technologizing of the Word.* NY: Methuen.

Chapter 11

Linguistics and the Historical Critical Method

Up to now this book has been investigating the impact of the contemporary language explosion on the study of the New Testament. This linguistic revolution is still in its early stages and its influence is still growing. It has encouraged a synchronic reading of the New Testament, that is, a concentration on the completed texts as they were received by the Church as its normative canon. This was the final stage and synthesis of a long period of tradition. The next chapter will look further into the New Testament as canon. Sociolinguistics studies how speakers and writers interact with language as a total system of signs at any given moment. Texts receive their meaning as part of that prevailing language world.

This approach to the New Testament in the context of how language works is an effort to complement the method of biblical studies presently prevailing in most seminaries and biblical faculties in universities. That is the so-called historical critical method. Historical criticism arose in response to the growth of self-consciousness that took place in western culture since the Enlightenment. The discovery of a way to decode tablets and inscriptions of ancient Near Eastern civilizations opened up insight into the social world that existed when the Jewish scriptures were being formed. Many similarities between the Bible and other ancient literatures were discovered.

Because proponents of the historical critical method were often motivated by rationalism and denied any uniqueness to the Jewish Bible, the Catholic Church and other conservative Christians originally resisted its methodology. Only in 1943 did Pope Pius XII cautiously accept its use. The Second Vatican Council incorporated a critical view of the formation of the Gospels into its Constitution on Revelation.

In many other Christian churches the historical critical method produced a split between liberal and fundamentalist wings. For some members it led to a loss of faith in the divine choice and guidance of Israel as God's chosen people. They came to look upon the Bible as one of many sets of popular religious documents from the ancient Near East and denied that it had any inspired character. The question of biblical inspiration will be treated in Chapters 21 and 22. For other believers — especially the early German scholars — historical critical studies were at home in the theological faculties of state universities to be developed freely, independent of any doctrinal control. These scholars focused attention on how the Bible developed diachronically, that is, on the historical development of traditions.

The historical critical method seeks to take readers "behind the text" and show them how it was formed and how it developed within a social community. Hans Frei, who investigated the principles and implications of this method during the eighteenth and nineteenth centuries, explains how it separated form from content. As applied to the New Testament, historical criticism tended to concentrate on recovering the historical Jesus. It pursued questions like: what kind of self-consciousness did he have? what did he actually teach? did he work miracles?

A common method of presenting the achievements of historical criticism in gospel studies is found in the Decree on Revelation of Vatican II. It envisions three stages leading to the production of the canonical Gospels, namely:

a) The period of the earthly ministry of Jesus. During that time Jesus experienced a religious call to proclaim the coming of God's Kingdom and devoted himself to preparing people for this imminent event. He did this by preaching, leaving no writings. As a result, Christians of later generations had no sources written in that period for ascertaining how Jesus viewed reality or what his understanding of God and the Kingdom was like. Above all, they have no record of the self-consciousness of the earthly Jesus, a topic of great interest today when Christians seek to understand the relation of Jesus to God as his father.

b) The period of the oral traditions. This period extends for more than a generation after the death of Jesus. His first followers knew that Jesus had been crucified. They also believed that God raised him from among the dead to make him Lord and Savior. These disciples became witness to this divine activity as the reality that promised to reconcile humanity to God. They founded eucharistic communities, that is, worshiping groups that celebrated the Lord's Supper to remember the death of Jesus as saving and that sought to obey his command of mutual unselfish love. This period was extremely active and gave rise to a wide range of local communities and theological traditions whose relationship to the earthly Jesus is not clear. During this time the first Christian writings began to appear. These included the letters of Paul, which deal with tensions existing in these communities. Short accounts of the mission of Jesus, liturgical hymns and collections of sayings of Jesus probably appeared also.

c) As the chosen apostles of Jesus began to die, leaders of the early churches felt the need of producing more substantial documents to keep the memory of Jesus alive. To Mark is given the credit of producing the first "gospel," that is an account of the ministry of Jesus in the light of God's approval of his obedience even to death (explained above in Chapter 6). The canonical Gospels embody primitive traditions from the oral period, but organize them according to the theological vision of the final editors or redactors. As such, the Gospels are not to be put into the category of chronicles. Yet their content and method of production are intertwined with the historical development of primitive Christian communities.

Out of this modern critical preoccupation with the historical truth of events narrated in the New Testament, especially in the canonical Gospels, arose several types of criticism, which account for divisions of New Testament studies today. The rest of this chapter will describe the important areas briefly, that is, it will present a description of the various forms of New Testament criticism as practiced today.

The methodology behind some of this criticism is not without controversy, and it has been attacked by Erhardt Güttgemanns at length. Werner Kelber has also called the value of this method into question in his careful investigation of the relation of oral tradition to the Gospel of Mark by concluding with this thesis: "the very form of gospel came into existence as a radical alternative to a tradition dominated by an oral ontology of language" (Kelber: 209). In other words, a written gospel is "a counterform to, rather than an extension of oral hermeneutics" (185).

AREAS OF NEW TESTAMENT CRITICISM

1. *Source Criticism*: study of the traditions and writings upon which the author relied in composing a text. Source criticism looks at elements like similarity in theme or vocabulary as well as common structure to postulate influence upon the author. It seeks to determine the kind and extent of this influence. An author has many choices in using sources: to accept, modify, combine or react against them. The sources may be treated as an adversary to be attacked and refuted. If an author is using sources and reacting dialectically to them and readers do not know this, then they cannot follow the argument of the text intelligently.

Example. Col 2:16-19 refers to a situation in the city of Colossae that has been disturbing and dividing the Christian community. In attacking this situation, Paul uses vocabulary that is part of the practices, which are not familiar to modern readers. This is what is involved in interpreting this passage and why commentators differ about what was happening.

All the sources used by the New Testament writers were not written. Only recently have biblical scholars started to take account of the special characteristics of oral sources with the understanding that: "The oral medium, in which words are managed from the mouth to the ear, handles information differently from the written medium, which links the eye to visible but silent letters on the page"(Kelber: xv). Study of oral traditions that preceded the text may shed light on the various types of criticism now being used to explain the formation of the gospels and other writings of the New Testament. In addition, historical critical studies must pay more attention to advances in the sociology of knowledge and sociolinguistics (Güttgemanns: 67-70; 170).

2. *Form Criticism*: study of the various kinds of literary units around which the gospels have been constructed. In the term "form criticism," form refers to the primary oral units employed during the various waves of Christian preaching. Form critics seek to determine the original social setting (technically called the Sitz im Leben) from which each distinct type of passage grew. Questions about them that form criticism addresses concern:

a) their point of origin — whether these forms go back to Jesus himself or to the oral teaching of disciples in the Aramaic speaking community of Jewish Christians, or to the Hellenistic segment of the emerging churches;

b) their original purpose — whether this form arose in controversy or liturgy or preaching or in a pastoral setting to justify a community practice, or in some other social setting;

c) their modification — whether the traditional form remained intact or was modified to meet changing conditions. Modifications include omissions, inserts or the combination of forms.

Example. Mark 11:27 — 12:40 preserves a series of controversies that reflect polemics between Jesus and his adversaries. Their arrangement by Mark is literary. Form criticism tries to discover the origin of each exchange.

3. *Redaction Criticism*, sometimes called *Editorial Criticism.* To supplement the minute analytical research of the form critics, who concentrate on the original primary units, redaction critics approach the canonical Gospels as complete literary unities. They look for evidence pointing to the personal input of the final redactor — also called editor or author — who made this book available to the community. Redaction critics are still uncovering literary indications of sophisticated input on the part of these final redactors. In the case of the Synoptic Gospels, their research is made easier by the existence of the large segments common to Matthew, Mark and Luke. In fact, that is why they are called "synoptic," a term to show that they can be seen in a single glance.

Research comparing the three Gospels is called the "synoptic problem," the solution to which still eludes centuries of investigation. The most common theory about their relationship is called the "two-source theory," namely that Matthew and Luke are mutually independent but both dependent on the Markan Gospel plus a second source, called Q, from the German word *Quelle*, meaning source.

Originally much form and redaction criticism was undertaken for dogmatic purposes: to affirm historical facts about the earthly life of Jesus. "Nineteenth century theology became dominated by the question of faith and history" (Davis: 274). Thus the following area of studies.

4. *Historical Criticism.* This is the aspect of criticism that seeks to determine exactly how much factual information can be retrieved from any given text. The whole concept of historical criticism of the New Testament is controversial because the members of the apostolic church did not have available for their use the technical form of critical history

now found in modern western civilization. Hence, no New Testament book is historical in the modern critical sense. Writers living at the time of Jesus were not preoccupied with objective historical accuracy. Hence the whole question of filtering out critical historical information about Jesus from the Gospels is problematic. In fact, to concentrate upon the four Gospels primarily as historical sources ignores the nature of their literary genre and runs the risk of misinterpreting them.

Hans Frei explains this point in technical language in his study of biblical interpretation during the eighteenth and nineteenth centuries. The conceptual mindset and theory of meaning "underlying historical criticism of the gospel narratives tends to move it away from every explanation of texts not directly governed by a referential theory of meaning or by the cognate identification of meaning with knowledge" (Frei: 135). He becomes more specific when he points out that German biblical scholars of the time were culturally unprepared to form "a critical appraisal of the differences and similarities between history and realistic fiction" (217). In fact, the whole movement of German biblical scholarship that shaped and dominated the growth of historical critical studies was not able to explain "the relation between words, descriptive shape and what they express" in biblical narratives (Frei: 308).

Why then did historical criticism flourish? Because Christians root their faith in the reality of the obedience of Jesus even unto his voluntary death for us. Accordingly, they searched for historical data to verify the contents of his teaching, the reality of his rejection by the leaders of his own people and the mystery of his transformed presence to the early Church. Such a quest became a significant part of New Testament studies in the face of the skeptics. This quest led to the publication of numerous lives of Jesus and treatises on christology that were written to supplement the scanty details of the Gospels.

Example. Luke 5:1-11 is a narrative of the call of Peter. It sees this call as coming after his taking in a wondrous catch of fish in obedience to the command of Jesus. But that event does not appear in the call of Peter described in Matt 4:18-22 or Mark 1:16-20. What really happened? Rather than being a historical corrective, this scene illustrates Luke's use of the widespread Greco-Roman theme of God as benefactor.

Once the books of the New Testament were written down, they were entrusted to the Christian community for its use in preaching and liturgical celebration. Until the invention of printing, each copy had to be made by hand — a true manuscript. As a result, thousands of scribal variations were incorporated into the copies of the texts that circulated. This condition created the need for the following critical discipline.

5. *Textual Criticism*: the technique of recovering the original text by a study of existing manuscripts. It is both an art and a science. New Testament textual criticism is unique because of the large number of extant Greek manuscripts (over 5,000, if the liturgical lectionaries are counted) plus the huge number of manuscripts of the versions (translations), especially from the Latin church. Many of these contain only one literary form, like a gospel or a letter. This means that the history of the manuscript tradition of different parts of the New Testament must be studied separately.

An important role of textual criticism is the editing of critical editions of the New Testament. These serve both as a basis for modern translations and as texts for commentaries. Making a critical edition entails three steps:

a) reviewing as many available manuscripts as possible;

b) grouping these manuscripts according to their place in the history of the manuscript tradition in order to decide to which text type and family within that type each one belongs. This shows their relationship to each other;

c) applying the rules worked out by textual critics for choosing the original reading in disputed passages.

6. *History of Exegesis.* The study of how the text was interpreted during successive periods of church history is another branch of New Testament criticism. In broad strokes, the history of exegesis (explanation of texts) falls into three periods:

a) the Patristic period, which was the age of homiletic commentaries — the sermons of the fathers of the Church. The two main schools of Patristic exegesis are the realistic and the allegorical. The realistic school, linked to the Syrian church and exemplified by St. John Chrysostom, took a common sense approach. It explained the literal sense as the primary meaning of the text. The allegorical school, associated with the church in Alexandria, borrowed heavily upon the allegorical techniques used to explain classical Greek myths. Its chief exponent was Origen, who strongly influenced St. Jerome and St. Augustine.

b) medieval scholastic exegesis. During this period the systematic study of theology flourished, and the Bible was studied with tools of rational analysis. Christian theologians had to study the homilies of the fathers, make "chains" of these, then write their own commentaries on the Bible before they were permitted to write their own theological syntheses (*summae*).

The most striking feature of medieval biblical exegesis was the development of the theory of the four senses of Scripture, flowing out of Paul's distinction between "letter and spirit" (see Chapter 7). The first and primary sense was the literal or first-order meaning, which St. Thomas Aquinas insisted was the basis of all other senses. The spiritual sense was divided into three types: allegorical, tropological and anagogic. The allegorical sense is the meaning that persons and events in the Old Testament had as types prefiguring and pointing to their fulfilment in the New Testament. The tropological or moral sense is the interpretation of scriptural texts in terms of the relation of the soul to God. The anagogic or eschatological sense is an interpretation of those events in Scripture that point to the final fulfilment in the heavenly kingdom.

Example. The city of Jerusalem was seen as having all four senses of Scripture. In the literal sense it was the actual city of David, the holy city, site of the Temple, center of true divine cult. In the allegorical sense it was a type of the New Covenant, the place of true and universal worship of God. In the tropological sense Jerusalem represented the human soul, called to be the chosen dwelling place of God and yet often rebelling against his will. In the anagogic sense it signified the glorious heavenly city.

c) the modern period — which is still in progress — is the period of scientific study of the Bible. It was during this period that the various scientific methods of New Testament criticism described here evolved. Out of these critical approaches grew up a special theological movement that has links to linguistics.

7. *Biblical Theology.* In the modern sense this movement began in Germany in the eighteenth century. It was an effort "to establish the unity of religious meaning across the gap of historical and cultural differences." It combined key themes, like that of a "developing history of religious ideas and outlook within the pages of the Bible with a conviction of God's special presence in the Bible" (Frei: 8). It assumed the existence of providence, a divine plan of salvation history and divine inspiration of the Bible. Since the validity of biblical theology depended upon the reality of the events of human salvation, like the mission of Jesus, it encouraged historical criticism as a means of verifying these events.

In this century the biblical theology movement has been challenged by various forms of contemporary philosophy. For example, Rudulf Bultmann's existential demythologizing is primarily concerned with what he considered the abiding truths that the Bible offers about the meaningfulness of human existence. The New Hermeneutic, a movement of biblical theology that flourished in the 1960s, grew out of Bultmann's existentialism, and especially his understanding of the resurrection of Jesus. "It is a method of approaching the problem of interpretation which has developed in full awareness of the historicality of human existence, and which seeks to find a viable way to cross the gap in meaning between the New Testament and our time" (Achtemeier: 23-24).

The goal of the New Hermeneutic was to attain to Jesus' own self-understanding by an existential theology of the word of God. By that method it hoped to solve the problem of the meaning of human existence. It looked to the word of God as the answer to widespread alienation among moderns because it saw "language as the key to man's existence" (Achtemeier: 24). The New Hermeneutic was introduced into the United States by students of Bultmann but never became a fruitful expression of biblical theology — in large measure because of its extreme individuality and its separation of meaning from linguistic performance. In fact, "Possibly the most fundamental criticism levelled against Bultmann's existential hermeneutic concerns his neglect of any reflection about language in general" (Bleicher: 106-107).

8. *Biblical philology.* Philology is the study of literary texts. Renewed interest in the word of God contributed to the production of important lexical tools for New Testament scholars, especially the lexicon of Walter Bauer. This valuable tool is available in a revised and updated English edition as *A Greek-English Lexicon of the New Testament and Other Early Christian Literature* by W. F. Arndt and F. B. Gingrich, augmented by Gingrich and F. W. Danker (U. of Chicago Press, 1979).

More controversial in terms of linguistic methodology, but also indispensable for New Testament word study, is the massive 10-volume lexicon begun by Gerhard Kittel to provide historical and linguistic background material for all key terms of the New Testament. It has been translated into English by Geoffrey W. Bromiley as the *Theological Dictionary of the New Testament* (Grand Rapids: Erdmans Publishing Co., 1964-1976). This monumental project ends with an essay on the nature of New Testament Greek and the problems of dealing with it in any dictionary — inserted as a gentle response to critics.

9. *Canonical Criticism.* As has been noted, the New Testament is the normative religious library guiding Christian belief and practice, rather than merely a collection of religious texts of purely historical interest. But how was this library or "canon" formed, and why are only certain books included by the Church? What criteria were used to admit some and reject others? These questions are linked to the authority that the New Testament enjoys. These questions are related to language in that canonical criticism sees the entire biblical canon as the context in which each of its books must be interpreted.

10. *Biblical Translation*, theory and practice. Biblical translation goes back before New Testament times. After the conquests of Alexander the Great, the Jews of the diaspora, that is, those Jews scattered among the Gentiles, could no longer read their Scriptures in Hebrew. They needed a Greek translation, and several were made. The most famous one was the so-called Septuagint (LXX), which dates from the second century B. C. It gets its name from the legend that it was translated by 70 elders sent by the Jewish high priest in Jerusalem to Alexandria to prepare a translation for the famous library there.

The New Testament books were the most widely translated writings in the ancient world. Early translations followed the establishment of local Christian communities in all parts of the civilized world. All of these translations were made according to the "formal" method, that is, translators followed the syntax of the original Greek text as closely as possible.

In modern times Eugene A. Nida, followed by other scholars of the United Bible Societies, has applied advances in linguistics to develop a new method, "dynamic equivalent translation." It works on the principle of the multilevel nature of language with its tension between the deep or semantic kernels and its surface grammatical structure. Dynamic equivalent translation first transforms the surface structure of the Greek text into its semantic kernels. These primary meaning units are then transformed into the receptor language (the modern language into which the translation is being made) and expressed in its surface structures. Thanks to this method, modern readers who are culturally flexible should be able to experience the same total appeal and impact felt by the original audience of the New Testament.

11. *New Testament Exegesis*: the art and science of explaining what the text said and meant for its original recipients. New Testament commentaries are composed to explain the content of one or more of its writings by applying the results of the various forms of criticism described in this chapter. They address different levels of audience and may appear individually or as part of a series. Shorter exegetical studies on individual passages of the New Testament text also appear in periodicals devoted to biblical and theological studies.

Readers can find what is being done in New Testament exegesis by consulting the standard annual bibliography of biblical research, the *Elenchus Bibliographicus Biblicus*, published by the Pontifical Biblical Institute in Rome. It is arranged systematically and includes the names of books, articles and even book reviews that deal with biblical topics in leading journals throughout the world.

Sources

Achtemeier, Paul J., 1969, *An Introduction to the New Hermeneutic*. Phila.: Westminster.

Bird, Phyllis A., 1982, *The Bible as the Church's Book*. Phila.: Westminster.

Bleicher, Josef, 1980, *Contemporary Hermeneutics: Hermeneutics as method, philosophy and critique*. Boston: Routledge & Kegan Paul.

Collins, Raymond F., 1977, "The Matrix of the New Testament Canon," *Biblical Theology Bulletin* 7:51-61.

Cumming, John and Burns, P., eds., 1981, *The Bible Now*. NY: Seabury.

Davis, Charles, 1982, "The Theological Career of Historical Criticism in the Bible," *Cross Currents* 32:267-284.

Frei, Hans W., 1974, *The Eclipse of Biblical Narrative: A Study of Eighteenth and Nineteenth Century Hermeneutics*. New Haven: Yale U. Press.

Güttgemanns, Erhardt, 1979, *Candid Questions Concerning Gospel Form Criticism*. Pittsburgh: Pickwick Press.

Harrington, Daniel J., 1979, *Interpreting the New Testament: A Practical Guide*. Wilmington: Michael Glazier.

Kelber, Werner H., 1983, *The Oral and Written Gospel*. Phila.: Fortress.

Reese, James M., 1983, "Perils of Proof-texting," *Biblical Theology Bulletin* 13:121-123.

Chapter 12

Language and
New Testament Culture

The momentum of historical consciousness expresses itself in the increasing complexity of the behavioral or — as the French say — "human sciences." Their ever widening impact is beginning to have noticeable influence upon New Testament studies by making commentators more sensitive to the eclectic culture that produced these writings. Modern readers cannot understand its books without some awareness of the complex world in which they were produced. Hence the current production of studies devoted to "the social sciences and the New Testament."

Some questions that social sciences, and particularly sociolinguistics, pose to the writings of the New Testament are: how would these texts have been received and understood by their original audience? what ideas and practices would that audience have resisted and rejected? what would they have found in it to celebrate? If reading is choice, how would these writings have changed their lives? From Chapter 7, which discussed theories about what takes place in reading, it is clear that "the understanding and interpretation of any sort of text is ultimately rooted in a social world, in a set of models sketching how the world works" (Malina, 1982: 231).

All commentators agree that the canonical New Testament was written entirely in Greek — no matter what the prehistory of its individual books. But did these works originate in a one-language structure world, like the modern United States, a two-language structure world, like Haiti with French and Haitian Creole, or even a three-language structure world, like Kenya, where many persons speak a native tribal language, Swahili for wider contacts and English to advance in political and intellectual prestige? Each of these cultural systems has its own social tensions (Nida, 1975b).

Furthermore, a distinction must be made between the language situation in the region where Jesus carried out his ministry and in places where New Testament authors like Paul and the evangelists completed their writing. No doubt Jesus usually spoke to his audience in Aramaic, a Semitic language related to Hebrew. By the time of Jesus Hebrew had become principally a liturgical language.

The writers of the early Christian communities, however, entered more into the cosmopolitan situation and adopted the common Greek of the period, a language that was in general use throughout the Roman Empire. These writers were influenced by the Septuagint translation of the Hebrew Bible (see Chapter 11), which had an impact on both the content and style of parts of the New Testament. Aramaic dialects of the period probably also influenced certain expressions found in it.

Example. Luke 1 — 2, the infancy gospel, was composed in conscious imitation of the style of the Greek Septuagint (LXX).

In light of such cultural data, a social studies model is gradually replacing the abstract approach of philosophical hermeneutics or method of approach, which divided New Testament interpretation into two stages: what the text meant in its original setting and what the text means to a modern audience. Linguists call these approaches the explicative and applicative. The newer model takes a trans-cultural approach that asks: how did the text reflect its original cultural setting, and then, how can this knowledge help modern readers translate its thrust into their social world?

The major obstacle to adopting this social studies model is the complexity of the problem. How can any single commentator grasp a whole social world, especially one that is far removed in many ways from modern western society? The social science method of constructing a theoretical model seeks to provide a simplified view of significant forces operative in the society under consideration. Chapter 3 gave an example of how this model approach functions in studying the analysis of a speech act as a unit of communication by Roman Jakobson. That model has transcultural application because all language groups exist to communicate.

In dealing with New Testament interpretation a further step must be kept in mind, namely, the different kinds of social institutions then existing. Readers have to learn how to transcend their modern viewpoint of a scientific world, for it colors their analysis of every class of relationships. They have to enter into the world view of that new class of people whose religious experience endured hostility to set up faith communities throughout the Roman Empire. Obviously language is the chief shaper and carrier of a people's world view. That is why this book devoted to explaining how to interpret the New Testament has spent so much time explaining how language works. But language and social institutions interact. Linguistics learns from cultural anthropology, sociology, sociolinguistics and the like, for they study relationships found in every society.

In keeping with the nature and complexity of the material studied by them, the behavioral sciences arrange their data according to the "functionalist, the conflict, and the symbolic models" (Malina, 1982: 233). These three models reflect the kinds of values at stake in any society. The functionalist models demonstrate the abiding relationships necessary for society to function predictably. And yet every society is in constant tension because its component groups are in the competition that generates change. Hence the need of conflict models. The symbolic models bring into bold relief goals, motivations, and values that "are attached to and embodied by persons, things, and events" at the time under consideration (Malina, 1982: 235).

Although models offer simplified views of complicated social situations, they do not have to be "reductionist." That is, they do not have to reduce complex situations so drastically that they fail to communicate the essential elements of the society they study. In the case of New Testament interpretation, the elements to be highlighted are essential features of both Hellenism and Judaism as they interacted with primitive Christians. This approach does not ignore the findings of the historical critical method discussed in Chapter 11, but it adds insights from transcultural anthropology to reduce the risk of bias in interpretation.

Anthropological studies of the society in which Jesus, Paul and the primitive Christian communities functioned reveal it to be a society in which religion was not a separate dimension of human existence. On the contrary, religion was embedded in either family or political life (Malina, 1981). Key features of the society were:

> a) the honor-shame tension, which was often manifest in the challenge and riposte dialogs in which Jesus engaged with his opponents. Unlike modern industrial societies, in which worth is evaluated in terms of wealth, the society in which Jesus lived was not oriented toward possessing or toward the rugged individualism of the self-made hero. It was a society in which worth was linked to honor in the eyes of one's fellows. In technical terms, individuals in such a society were said to have a "dyadic personality." This phrase "describes individuals as embedded with the group and their behavior as determined by significant others" (Harrington: 186).

> Example. Mark 12:13-17. When Jesus challenged his fellow teachers among the Pharisees to answer one of the important questions about maintaining Jewish honor in a society under foreign domination, he vindicates his honor and offers hope to his fellow Israelites because of his wisdom.

72670

b) limited-goods model. The society in which Jesus lived did not possess unlimited resources. Production of goods and services was strictly limited. Possessors had to exchange their talents and resources for what they needed from others. In that situation, economics was not a formal independent institution but part of the community's communal values and relationships.

Example. Luke 14:12-14. When Jesus tells his followers to invite those "who do not possess anything to give you in return," he is outlining a new set of values that will prevail in the Kingdom of God.

c) patron-client relationship. The universal interdependence of a society based on limited resources demanded that all members be linked as patrons or clients. Since every segment of society needed all the others, networks of interdependence grew up between the various kinds of patrons, who were able to offer one type of service, and clients, who could offer another type. Their mutual support kept society functioning stably.

Example. Luke 16:5-7. The parable deals with the activities of the manager of an estate owned by an absentee landlord. He seizes an opportunity to manipulate accounts of clients to insure his own survival.

The application of insights from the social sciences to New Testament studies still must prove its value as a tool for interpretation. "The value of the sociological approach will be proved primarily by its ability to illumine obscure texts and to provide insight into the social situations in which Christianity arose and developed" (Harrington: 190).

How do the cultural dimensions of the prevailing society touch upon the language of the New Testament writings? Speaking as an anthropologist-linguist, Eugene Nida states that the semantic structure of language has links to "culturally significant attitudes and beliefs." This linkage is not reflected in the surface structures of language, which are "frozen" and change slowly. What is operative in the way people explain and classify reality is that "most taxonomic relations in semantics represent the current beliefs" (Nida: 1975a: 89). Semantic taxonomy refers to the way a group classifies its meaning system, how attitudes and beliefs interrelate and influence actions.

Attention to cultural relations prevailing within the social groups out of which the New Testament writings sprang not only demands acquaintance with the language explosion but also contributes to its effect by shedding light on the cultural dimensions of meaning. Words are dynamic expressions of culture, symbols of its elements. In this respect, knowledge of the prevailing culture is necessary to understand its "technical" words like Pharisee, Samaritan, priest, espoused, and also its common words like boat, shepherd, oil.

The social conditions of the early Christian communities also influenced the ways in which the New Testament writings were circulated, collected, edited, and eventually preserved as the Church's authoritative or normative apostolic library. "Viewed from the perspective of the sociology of knowledge, the prolonged debates about the contents of the New Testament canon as well as the end result of these debates, the New Testament in its present form, must be seen as part of the efforts of the early churches to construct and maintain a symbolic universe in harmony with the changing social circumstances of Christianity from the second through the fourth centuries A.D." (Gager: 265).

Sources

Gager, John G., 1982, "Shall We Marry Our Enemies? Sociology and the New Testament," *Interpretation* 37:256-265.

Harrington, Daniel J., 1980, "Sociological Concepts in the Early Church: A Decade of Research," *Theological Studies* 41: 181-190.

Malina, Bruce, 1981, *The New Testament World: Insights from Cultural Anthropology*. Atlanta, John Knox.

Malina, Bruce, 1982, "The Social Sciences and Biblical Interpretation," *Interpretation* 37: 229-242.

_____1983, "Why Interpret the Bible with the Social Sciences?" *American Baptist Quarterly* 2: 119-133.

Nida, Eugene A., 1975a, *Componential Analysis of Meaning*. The Hague: Mouton.

_____1975b, *Language Structure and Translation*. Stanford: Stanford U. Press.

Nida, Eugene A. and Reyburn, William D. ,1981, *Meaning Across Culture*. Maryknoll, NY: Orbis Press.

Conclusion to Part I

The vastness of this effort to apply advances in linguistics and semiotics to a study of the New Testament may overwhelm students — and even teachers — but their initial wonder can be fruitful if directed along productive lines. I want to remind readers that they cannot keep up with all speculation about language. They do not have to know all the details to find nourishment in the inspired text.

Believers read the New Testament as members of a Christian community whose composite interests, wisdom, needs and concerns enable members to build one another up in the task of understanding and responding to its message. In fact, a willingness to draw on the insights of others — not to reinvent the wheel — is the most important support to be gained from the variety of methods being put forth in all forms of linguistics. Each of the prevailing dimensions of criticism can deepen appreciation for the value of interdisciplinary study of the New Testament. To sum up briefly (see Suleiman), the method proposed thus far embraces such varied criticisms as:

— sociological, in its variety of forms, to locate texts in their social world by making use of models;
— rhetorical, with its analysis of language levels and its skill in choosing words and organizing textual units;
— hermeneutical or interpretative, for focusing attention on the philosophical issues to which the text speaks;

— audience oriented, to utilize reader participation to explore new applications in today's world;

— semiotic, that reinforces the insights of structuralism to illustrate how linguistic signs have power to continue to generate new meaning;

— phenomenological, with its power to incorporate all manifestations of human endeavors within a transcendent synthesis;

— impressionistic and psychoanalytic, that utilize images and symbols as keys to open the hidden resources of the human psyche.

The linguistics that holds a society together is not an abstraction. Continued research on Jakobson's analysis of the speech act or communication event shows the complexity of the interaction between all elements and functions involved. Humans communicate and share truth and values in an amazing variety of ways. It is to these values and to these special shared truths embodied in the New Testament that Part II of this book will now turn.

The linguistic investigation of Part I provides the foundation for studying the religious dimension of the New Testament. That dimension involves images and symbols, what Amos Wilder calls a "theopoetic." To grasp these, Part II will investigate religious imagination. How can this new Christian language be appropriated once more by those who seek to respond to God's salvation in Jesus Christ?

Source

Suleiman, Susan R. and Crosman, Inge, eds., 1980, *The Reader in the Text: Essays on Audience and Interpretation*. Princeton: Princeton U. Press.

Part II

Religious Language and Imagination

Chapter 13

Theolinguistics: Understanding Religious Language

Efforts to read the New Testament as the liturgical library and normative Scripture of the Christian Church require some knowledge of how language communicates and of what demands reading makes. In addition, to understand these writings is to enter the conceptual world or the "universe of discourse" that produced these books and which they help to maintain for believers.

Christians want not only to seek life through these texts for themselves. They also want to share the vision of reality they receive from the New Testament with their contemporaries in religious dialog. They see it not only as a system of language but as a way of life, a force for peace and justice in the world.

Up to this point my study has dealt with general principles of language and semiotics that apply to all texts, specifying them by examples taken from the New Testament. Now it is time to explain how this library of texts is able to communicate the unique religious experience created by the Christ event to the believers of today. This religious experience created a new language, a Christian theolinguistics. If they want to commune with these writings and make them meaningful, "theologians should not work with obsolete conceptions of language" (van Noppen: 2).

To enable believers to communicate with modern society, Christian anthropologists-linguists like Eugene Nida are developing the discipline of theolinguistics, a "pluridisciplinary field of investigation offered by the linguistic articulation of religious belief and thought" (van Noppen: 1). In doing so they carry out the hope that Pope Paul VI saw as guiding Christian interpreters of Scripture. He reminded them that it is not enough to be faithful to the text that they explain. They must also be faithful to those to whom they explain the biblical text today. Only in this double fidelity can they make the Bible a source of meaningful answers to real human needs (see Chapter 19). Modern believers live in a different conceptual world than that of Jesus and the early Christians. The New Testament is in many ways foreign to modern ways of thinking.

The chapters of Part II of this study will focus on reasons for this change and elaborate on the method devised by Amos N. Wilder to deal with the problems involved for interpreting the New Testament. He calls this method "theopoetic," namely, a creative application of religious imagination according to valid canons of literary criticism. This chapter will discuss features of religious language or "theolinguistics" as a preliminary step. It enables serious students of the New Testament to understand why modern culture places many obstacles in the way of hearing and responding to the inspired text.

Like other forms of language, theolinguistics is employed primarily for communicating. It has the factors and functions of communication events or speech acts analyzed by Roman Jakobson and explained above in Chapters 3 and 4. In religious language the dominant element is the expressive, an articulation of the experience of the God-ward thrust of communication. This language operates simultaneously on many levels, that is, it is polyvalent: it embraces not only understanding but also imagination, emotion and response.

Amos Wilder has spent his long teaching and writing career warning against the reduction of Christian religious language to sentiment or to acts of the will alone to the neglect of reason and imagination. "If revelation has to speak against culture, it has also to speak through it and by it" (Wilder: 209). New Testament readers today are obliged to bridge the gap between cultures. Its text makes use of the symbols and mythopoetic features of the Jewish culture to nourish wills of persons instructed by the revelation of Moses, the prophets, the sages and Jesus. Its symbolism is permeated by all dimensions of human experience as shaped by its traditions: personal and social, sensual and conceptual, male and female, enslaved and free.

The Christian Church depends upon these texts to support its public worship, its private prayer and its moral practice. Like all language, New Testament terminology can become stale, superficial and even deceitful if its readers are not kept animated by the ongoing experience of the world it celebrates. How can they keep in touch with plastic features of its living word as a means of being faithful to its saving power?

Because of the cultural gap between the events that brought the New Testament into being and the needs of modern readers, today's readers do not automatically grasp its symbolic and imaginative religious language. To bridge that gap provides the program for the remaining chapters of this book. Even a solid linguistic methodology is not enough to enable readers to find nourishment for faith in the New Testament. Part of the challenge of religious texts is to communicate their paradoxical vision of reality and to arouse a taste for mystery. Such an attitude is necessary to hear texts like the parables of Jesus, which communicate the mystery of the Kingdom of God (see Reese). Faith shows humans that they are more citizens of that kingdom than of this world that is passing away. The Bible dramatizes the tensions between these two worlds. First attempts to draw insight and guidance from writings filled with paradox, mystery and strange situations may result in confusion and discouragement. Modern believers are often tempted to read about the New Testament rather than to dialog directly with its text.

Theolinguistics undertakes the task of showing how to understand the qualities of the New Testament world that ground its text. Four features of that world that are also manifest in its vocabulary, style and literary forms are:

1) The New Testament employs limit language, that is, it deals with the ultimate goals of human striving. In technical terms, it has a transcendent referent. This means that it holds out to believers a goal beyond the power of purely human strength. All of its language refers to God, who has revealed himself in and through Jesus Christ. "No one has ever seen God" (John 1:18). Readers can accept this language only by faith in God's revelation. This means to acknowledge God as unique referent, not as one subject among many others vying for our loyalty. As the Father of Jesus, God guarantees the significance of the religious affirmations of the New Testament and guards those who entrust themselves to its word from deception. At the same time, moreover, since God is transcendent, to confess him as God is not the same as making statements about creatures (see Chapter 17).

In theological terms, statements about God are analogous, that is, they reveal God only to a limited degree, proportionate to human capacity to understand. Human religious statements share a dimension of reality that does not fit into the ordinary categories of human divisions. Rather than dealing with God in abstract terms, religious truth is best expressed in the concrete images of symbols. Symbols point to the transcendent God as the limit of human striving, as wisdom and power beyond definition. And yet this divine presence is nearer to us than we are to ourselves.

2) New Testament religious language is social and universal, the language of the "new creation" (Gal 6:15). God intervenes in Jesus Christ to break down human barriers and to raise up for himself "a chosen people, enthusiastic for good works" (Titus 2:14).

3) The New Testament world is rooted in an unfolding saving plan conceived by the Father of Jesus Christ as a blessing for all humanity. The first three chapters of the Letter to the Ephesians celebrate this "mysterious plan" in sonorous liturgical phrases as the economy of God's grace and loving favor. It was proclaimed by the apostles chosen by Jesus and by the wandering charismatic prophets of the early Church (Eph 3:2-7). Sharing in this plan and in its benefits is not determined by race but by faith in Jesus Christ, a faith that translates into the works of mutual love. Only when that love reigns supreme will "God's design in its entirety" come to fulfilment (Acts 20:27).

4) The specifying feature of this saving plan of God is its form as the "New Covenant" in the blood of Christ, the New Covenant of thanksgiving which is celebrated by the living out of the eucharistic meal that proclaims the death of Jesus until he comes again in glory (1 Cor 11:26). The sacramental activity of the Church is empowered by the gift of the indwelling Holy Spirit of the crucified and risen Jesus so that it can bear witness to its saving Lord throughout human history.

The apostolic Church handed down the inspired account of this saving plan in the literary forms discussed above in Chapter 6. These writings employ the plastic forms of symbolic and mythopoetic language available to the Christian community from the Jewish Scriptures, from which most of New Testament imagery is derived. Like all images, those of the Bible have their origin in a concrete time-conditioned culture. Hence they have the historical limitations of every human language and need to be explained to modern readers by the methods of transcultural sociolinguistics. In many ways modern western readers regard language that relies heavily upon images as less meaningful than the exact language of scientific expression. "God-language is regarded as relative, depending on place, time, means of production and subsistence, changes in social experience" (Dillistone: 9). In this sense the language of the gospels can be called "transitional." It must always be related to the problems and questions of the age to which its saving message is preached.

No wonder then that Christian theologians of every age began to translate the New Testament revelation into the various rational systems of thought that dressed God's saving plan in conceptual terms and systems. Theologizing is necessary for the human spirit, but all valid systematic Christian theology has its roots in the language, images and symbols of the New Testament. Organized communities need systematic presentations to catechize new members in the gospel, because the human mind wishes to know and must synthesize to know. A good example of organizing Paul's pastoral anthropology is *Becoming Human Together* by Jerome Murphy-O'Connor, a professor at the Dominican Ecole Biblique in Jerusalem. Paul Ricoeur, who coined the famous maxim, "The image gives rise to thought," can reflect on what it means "To name God."

But the believing community must also keep up a living contact with its primary religious texts — what Christians call the Old and New Testaments — if it is to continue to bear witness to the saving plan of God in Christ Jesus. This task of growing in more fruitful understanding of the New Testament is what guides the study of the development of human religious imagination, which will be treated in the next three chapters. Through religious imagination or "theopoesis," believers synthesize the many levels of religious experience that form the subject matter of the Christ event.

Sources

Dillistone, F. W., 1981, "Attitudes to Religious Language," in van Noppen (see below), 5-21.

Murphy-O'Connor, Jerome, 1982, *Becoming Human Together: The Pastoral Anthropology of St. Paul.* Wilmington: Michael Glazier.

Prince, Gerald, 1980, "Notes on the Text as Reader," in Susan R. Suleiman and Inge Crosman, eds.,

The Reader in the Text. Princeton: Princeton U. Press

Reese, James M., 1975, *Preaching God's Burning Word*. Collegeville: Liturgical Press.

Ricoeur, Paul, 1981, "Nommer Dieu," in van Noppen (see below), 343-367.

Van Noppen, Jean-Pierre, ed., 1981, *Theolinguistics*. Brussels: Vrije Universteit, N.S. 8.

Wilder, Amos N., 1964, "The Word as Address and the Word as Meaning," in J. M. Robinson and J.B. Cobb, Jr., eds., *The New Hermeneutics*. NY: Harper and Row, 198-218.

Chapter 14

Imagination in Greek, Latin, Scholastic and Renaissance Writing

The Christ event was a unique moment in world history and evoked a new language that eventually became embodied in the New Testament, which is composed in a religious "nonpropositional, event-verbalizing," symbolic language. "Regaining a sense of awe before the imaginative discourse of creative primitive Christianity, commentators sensitive to this new language want to give the text its own voice" (Doty: 151). To do this it is necessary to locate the language of the New Testament within the flow of the history of the development of human self-consciousness. I propose to do so over the next three chapters by giving a brief history of how the understanding of imagination developed. This development will show why the theopoetic or religious imagination has a significant part to play in recovering a sense of the transforming power of the New Testament for Christian life today.

Believers are still seeking to recover that common universe of discourse "that was shattered with the rise of modern sensibility" during the Renaissance. "Because we inherit

a postmedieval fissure between literal and symbolic meaning," we have to find a way to relate in a meaningful way to
the cultural world in which the New Testament came into
being (Altizer: 24). But why adopt the route of the imagination if "what we know as the imagination is a distinctively
modern historical phenomenon," in fact, one that is
"uniquely Western in both its form and content" (Altizer:
19, 21)? The answer can be found in the achievements of a
transcultural approach that recognizes the world of Jesus
and the first Christians as being different from ours.

Modern cognitive psychology has been concerned with
the "imagination as a phenonomon within our cognitive
system." Its research recognizes that "one characteristic of
the imaginative process is its property of creating an alternative environment...another living space in which one can
perform and process information" (Singer: 20). Traces of
this process appear in ancient writing, although a full development of its role had to wait until modern times. "Since the
days of the ancient Greeks or of the Chinese philosophers
who flourished in the same period approximately 2500 years
ago, it has been apparent that human beings have recognized the existence of a special experience which we label
imagination" (Singer: 5).

Such insights of cognitive psychology are an important
corrective to the selective approach of the theologian Altizer
in guiding our examination of the growth of imaginative
language. As stated in the last chapter, religious language is
self-involving; it is the language of commitment and self-
transcendence. It is the way humans acknowledge that they
are dependent beings, responsible to a higher power, without which they could not exist. In philosophy this reality is
treated in the fundamental question of the relation of the
one and the many. That mysterious relationship raises the
question of how human beings know: how do they draw
what is "out there" into their minds?

Attempts to answer that question led Aristotle to propose
a complex model of the human mind with a dual set of
cognitive powers: one on the sensitive and the other on the
rational level. In between these two levels he postulated the

existence of a mediating faculty to coordinate the sensing and the thinking powers. The role of this mediating faculty was somehow to transform the multiple sense images into more refined images or phantasms that could be handled by the rational part of the mind. This power Aristotle called the *phantasia*, which is usually translated as "imagination." However, he did not develop this insight at any length in his tract *On the Soul*, nor did he integrate it fully into his theory of knowledge. As a result, commentators are not in agreement about how Aristotle understood the role of the imagination as mediating between sensing and thinking (Franks).

Since the imagination performed a task beyond that of the external senses, it played an important role in sense perception. It was a movement resulting from the activation of the sensitive powers of the soul and remained an organ of the sensitive part of the soul. Although he assigned it an essential step in preparing data received from the external senses for use by the rational faculty of the soul, Aristotle also considered imagination to be a dangerous faculty. It caused error if it failed to arrange the images it abstracted from the senses correctly (*On the Soul* 427-429). This fear remained prominent in the teaching on the imagination in the tradition that followed Aristotle during the Patristic and scholastic periods.

In his *Republic* Plato proposed four kinds of knowledge in the human mind, one of which was *eikasia*, the activity of knowing images. But he never conceived of this form of "imagination" as a special faculty, nor did he develop an analysis of the knowing process.

With the breakdown of classical Greek civilization after the death of Alexander the Great (323 B.C.), Greek philosophy turned more into a medley of self-help systems of theosophy and did not offer any new insights into human psychology. Nor did Latin philosophy. The Latin term *imaginatio* scarcely appears in the golden age of Latin literature. Roman philosophers — the few times they mention the term — ordinarily use the transliterated Greek *phantasia*.

Two essentials to be retained from this brief summary of the classical period are: 1) imagination was a subordinate part of the single human knowing process, which embraced the entire range of knowing from sense perception to discursive thinking. It was distinct both from sensation, which engages the world passively, and from appetite and judgment, which engage the world actively. 2) imagination was purely reproductive, that is, although it could rearrange images, and in so doing form new perceptions, it could not create any new concept.

Neither Greek word for imagination appears in the New Testament, although the Revised Standard Version employs the word once. In Luke 1:51, the term *dianoia* (thought) is translated imagination. Yet, the New Testament is full of imaginative and symbolic language. Hence, interpreters should be sensitive to this plastic language and relate it to contemporary needs in Christian life today (Musurillo: 3).

The philosopher Plotinus (c. 205-270 A.D.) viewed the imagination, which he called the *phantastikon*, as part of the sensitive soul, between the vegetative soul and reason. Its special power was to lay hold of objects and make them part of the self so that it was "the *terminus ad quem* of all properly human experience," without which humans could have "no conscious experience" (Warren: 277). Its role was to be "an intimate link that holds the various operations of the human soul together" (279). Plotinus seems to have conceived of two human souls in each person, held together by the synthesizing grasp of an imagination that guaranteed a single human consciousness.

This line of reasoning appears to form a link to the account of imagination as understood by the Arab mystic of Ṣūfism, Ibn 'Arabī. Imagination belongs to "an intermediate world, the world of Idea-Images, of archetypal figures, of subtle substances, of 'immaterial matter'" (Corbin: 4). Ṣūfism was a "unique conjunction between prophetic religion and mystical religion" (Corbin: 7). It posited the existence of "the active Imagination, the organ which at once produces symbols and apprehends them (14). Ṣūfism viewed imagination also as an intermediary, but between "the world of Mystery" and "the world of visibility." It was "the place of apparition" of spiritual beings (189), that is, it belonged to the world of archetypes, of divine active imagination. The approach of Ibn 'Arabī was mystical and resulted in a theosophical system that lay between the orthodox religious paradoxes of Islam and western concepts of monism (Corbin: 190-207). He postulated in humans an active, "theophanic" imagination that accomplishes at every moment a "new creation" and in so doing reveals the divine. His teaching on the "science of the Imagination" celebrates "the creativity of the heart" capable of receiving divine revelation (216-245).

In dealing with the imagination St. Thomas Aquinas remained within his role as commentator on the psychology of Aristotle. Although he used the term 721 times throughout his writings, he accepts Aristotle's approach completely and locates the imagination within the sensitive part of the soul; it never goes beyond the function of abstracting from the senses. St. Thomas does refer in passing to the works of Arabic philosophers who called the working of the intellect "imagination of intellect" (*De Veritate* 1.14.1) That reference shows that he knew about the tradition of imagination that developed in the neo-Platonic mysticism of Plotinus.

During the Patristic era the Platonist worldview, mingled with "a strong magical component," continued and was influential in forming the dualist understanding of imagination of the Renaissance. "Thus, at times imagination is extolled as the divine spark in man/woman, at others is the ultimate vindication of human potential" (Joy: 46-47).

The short survey about how imagination was conceived before modern times helps us appreciate the change in self-consciousness that came about during the Romantic period. That transition will be the topic of the next chapter.

Sources

Altizer, Thomas J., 1981, "The Apocalyptic Identity of the Modern Imagination," in Charles E. Winquist, ed., *The Archeology of the Imagination: Journal of the American Academy of Religion. Thematic Studies 48/2: 19-29.*

Corbin, Henry, 1969, *Creative Imagination in the Ṣūfism of Ibn the 'Arabī.* Princeton: Princeton U. Press.

Doty, William G., 1972, *Contemporary New Testament Interpretation.* Englewood Cliffs, NJ: Prentice-Hall.

Franks, Joan Marie, 1981, *The Role of Imagination in Aristotle's Account of Thinking.* U. of Toronto: Ph. D. Dissertation.

Joy, Morny, 1983, "Explorations in the Philosophy of Imagination: The Work of Gilbert Durand and Paul Ricoeur," in John V. Apczynski, ed., *Foundations of Religious Literacy.* Chico, CA: Scholars Press, 45-58.

Musurillo, Hubert, 1962, *Symbolism and the Christian Imagination.* Dublin: Helicon.

Singer, Jerome L., 1981, "Towards the Scientific Study of Imagination," *Imagination, Cognition and Personality* 1:5-28.

Warren, E. W., 1966, "Imagination and Plotinus," *Classical Quarterly* 60:277-285.

Chapter 15

Growth of Modern Concepts of Imagination in the Romantic Period

The first uses of the term "imagination" in English occur in the fourteenth century. They refer to the mental faculty for forming images or to the image-making process itself. Shakespeare gives an early hint of the modern meaning that grew out of the Renaissance only in one passage, namely in Act V of *A Midsummer Night's Dream*, although he used the term in its medieval sense elsewhere. In this new sense he speaks of imagination as a property of lunatics, lovers and poets; it makes them "apprehend more than cool reason ever comprehends." Its activity is creative but its results vary from producing the fantasies of lunatics to forming the new worlds of poets (Altizer: 19).

Thomas Hobbes (1588-1679) provided some psychological direction for reflecting on imagination in his theory of artistic creation (Brett: 11). John Locke's "new model of the mind," which equated thought with sensations that impress themselves on the mind as "simple ideas," influenced the "revolutionary changes in the idea of imagination." But, curiously enough, these changes appeared only gradually during the Romantic period. For Locke, "thought is seeing," and imagination is "the very medium of all thought"

(Tuveson: 21). The Romantic critics took an unexpectedly long time to implement their growing insights on creative imagination.

Not until Joseph Addison (1672-1719) did a treatise "on aesthetics as a wholly autonomous subject" appear (Tuveson: 92). This was his long essay on "The Pleasures of the Imagination," which was published in the form of columns 411-421 in the *Spectator*, June 21-July 21, 1712. For the first time, poetic imagination was divorced from reason and presented as producing its own effect, namely, pleasure. Addison held that "beauty, goodness, and truth inhabit separate compartments of the mind," and that they represent autonomous and equal functions of the personality (81). No longer did pleasure have to be ranked as servant of reason.

An aesthetic revolution occurred as the result of the many forces at work in the western world in the wake of the Renaissance and the Protestant Reformation. Tuveson summarizes these effects broadly under two headings: a) investigations into the nature and working of the human mind; b) the new idea of the cosmos that emerged (Tuveson: 2). This revolution, which produced an axial change in human self-consciousness, had a profound impact on all of modern life. It must be taken into consideration for the interpretation of the New Testament today. The Romantic movement generated enthusiasm for Nature as "the symbol of new hope." Instead of the classical approach to understanding nature in terms of revelation, by a new "physiotheology" revelation was understood in terms of Nature (Tuveson: 56-61).

One of the most influential voices of the Romantic movement was Samuel Taylor Coleridge (1772-1834). He gives a short philosophical definition of imagination in Chapter 13 of his *Biographia Literaria*, entitled, "For the Imagination or Esemplastic Power" (a term he coined from the Greek phrase for making a single image). He prepared for this summary by ten theses to prove the existence of "the absolute I AM" against "the Theists of the mechanic school." Coleridge identified himself as a believing Christian for whom "true metaphysics are nothing else but true divinity."

Because he objected to "the vagueness or insufficiency of the terms used in the metaphysical schools of France and Great Britain since the revolution," he felt the need to summarize his metaphysics before writing about imagination.

Already in Chapter 4 of his *Biographia* Coleridge wrote that after making repeated meditations he concluded, "Fancy and Imagination were two distinct and widely different faculties." On the advice of a friend he reduced Chapter 13 to a mere summary of his original plan. Its present form contains only the definitions of two types of imagination: 1) Primary — the living power and prime agent of all human perception, and as a repetition in the finite mind of the eternal act of creation in the infinite I AM." 2) Secondary — "an echo of the former, coexisting with the conscious will." That is, both are of the same "kind" and differ "only in *degree* and in the *mode* of operation." Coulson identifies the secondary with the literary imagination (10).

Coleridge speaks of imagination as essentially vital. "It dissolves, diffuses, dissipates, in order to recreate." By contrast, fancy, which simply "fixities and definites," is a mode of memory "emancipated from the order of time and space." Only by the study of his *Notebooks* is it possible to appreciate his use of the term imagination, upon which he made religion depend, even as he saw imagination dependent upon religion. Hence, his criticism is simultaneously literary, social and theological, for Scripture was "the living *educts* of the Imagination" (Coulson: 12-14). At the end of Chapter 14, Coleridge calls imagination the soul of poetic genius that forms all qualities (good sense, fancy, motion) "into one graceful and intelligent whole."

The mention by Coleridge of the "mechanic school" is a reminder that Romanticism was in part a reaction to Newton's view of the universe that prevailed among scientists from the eighteenth until this century. The universe was a fixed mechanical system. When reason was reduced to analysis, "The function of imagination increased in power and importance" (Welsh: 15). In general, theologians accepted this view of physical reality and looked upon God as the designer of the universe.

To escape this closed system, the Romantics latched onto the idea of imagination, which they used in a variety of ways. Yet, they achieved no common understanding of the term, so that Tuveson complains, "It is frustrating to attempt to talk of 'imagination' in the Renaissance and 'imagination' in the nineteenth century in common terms" (Tuveson: 95). By 1850, "the word 'imagination' had become so overworked" that it was used to cover "numerous and contradictory attitudes" (148).

By popularizing the notion of human creativity, the French Encyclopedists encouraged those who generalized the creative imagination into the "sole active power of the human mind" (Welsh: 68). The author who provided the philosophical base for the "conception of the imagination as poetic and as relatively autonomous" was Immanuel Kant (1724-1804) (Casey: 58). In his *Critique of Judgment* he "was the first to give a clear and convincing proof of the autonomy of art," a subject that up to that time was placed under theoretical knowledge or moral life (Cassirer: 137).

Kant posited three levels or kinds of imagination: 1) the reproductive — as noted above, the only type that Aristotle conceived of; 2) the productive — located between sense perception and the understanding, and enabling the understanding to do discursive reasoning; 3) the aesthetic — a blind but indispensale faculty that serves reason by mediating between it and the understanding through symbols. At every level the role of the imagination is to synthesize, that is, to gather, examine and connect the variety of pure intuitions to produce knowledge out of them (*Critique of Pure Reason*, B 103).

The way that use of the term expanded is dramatically illustrated by William Blake (1757-1824). In an aside — found both in *Milton* (plate 3, lines 3-4) and *Jerusalem* (Plate 5, lines 58-59) — he speaks of "Imagination, which is the Divine Body of the Lord Jesus," thus identifying it as source of divine revelation. He arrives at that point from his apocalyptic approach, "even creating a new literary genre" that recovered the apocalyptic identity of Jesus, anticipating "thereby a historical discovery which occurred some three generations later" (Altizer: 22-23).

The eighteenth and nineteenth centuries saw nothing less than a philosophical reconstruction of human nature. Witness their variety of theories on the nonrational faculties of human beings. Welsh reduces this complex development to three schools, according to the way each viewed the productive powers of humans (Welsh: 85-106). These human powers were seen as belonging: 1) to Reason alone — the opinion of poets like Coleridge and Emerson; 2) to both Reason and Imagination — the opinion of philosophers like Kant and Hegel; 3) to the Imagination alone — a minority opinion, one held by Schopenhauer, who affirmed that "man's greatest and only substantial power is imagination, insight, vision" (Welsh: 120).

This reconstruction of reflection on the essence of human nature gave rise to new forms of faith. It also caused a reaction among Catholic apologists seeking to express their tradition in a form that spoke to their contemporaries. One of the most famous of these apologists was John Henry Newman (1801-1890), who even located certitude in the imagination. In the earlier drafts of his *Grammar of Assent*, Newman distinguished between "the notional assent being languid, and the imaginative being energetic." This "imaginative assent" was later changed to "real." It was the assent that always addressed a "world," in much the same sense that a novelist builds a world (Coulson: 59-70). At the same time Newman clung to his insistence that believers must preserve the "words and ordinances" of revelation: "there being nothing else given us by which to ascertain or enter into it" (Coulson: 75). His own style was a fruitful marriage of disciplined rhetoric and dynamic religious imagination.

Along with the support it gives to preserving traditional language, the imagination can "release new meanings by dissipating old ones." The Church is a linguistic community recognized and bonded by its common language, formed by its liturgy, nourished by its Scripture and perfected by living in Christ (Coulson: 162). Newman saw the Church as losing ground because it yielded too much to the methods of science rather than celebrating the beauties of its traditional faith as found in the writings of the Fathers, who communicated in the language of metaphor, story and symbol.

The ever increasing celebration of the imagination from the Renaissance went hand in hand with the growing self-consciousness of human beings. Their wide-ranging reflections on the imagination during the Romantic age prepared the way for the "discovery" of the unconscious. The ongoing fascination with the unconscious in turn continues to feed the contemporary exaltation of the imagination and to foster insights as to its impact on biblical studies. The following chapter will deal with this topic in terms of recent speculation in "the human sciences."

Sources

Altizer, Thomas J., 1981, "The Apocalyptic Identity of the Modern Imagination," in C. E. Winquist, ed., *The Archeology of Imagination: Journal of the American Academy of Religion. Thematic Studies* 48/2: 19-29.

Brett, R. L., 1969, *Fancy and Imagination.* London: Methuen.

Casey, Edward S., 1967, *Poetry and Ontology: A Study of the Poetic Imagination, Poetic Language, and the Imaginary.* Evanston: Northwestern U. Dissertation.

Cassirer, Ernst, 1944, *An Essay on Man: An Introduction to a Philosophy on Human Culture.* New Haven: Yale U. Press.

Coulson, John, 1981, *Religion and Imagination:"In aid of a grammar of assent."* Oxford: Clarendon Press.

Maritain, Jacques, 1955, "The Experience of the Poet," *The Situation of Poetry.* NY: Philosophical Library.

Tuveson, Ernest Lee, 1960, *The Imagination as a Means of Grace: Locke and the Aesthetics of Romanticism.* Berkeley: U. of California Press.

Warnock, Mary, 1976, *Imagination.* Berkeley: U. of California Press.

Welsh, Livingston, 1935, *Imagination and Human Nature.* Cambridge: R. I. Severs.

Chapter 16

Contemporary Plurality
in Describing the Imagination

The brief review of research on the history of the imagination given in the last two chapters shows the growing importance and complexity of the topic. Lack of uniformity in vocabulary for describing the nature and function of the imagination reflects the variety of approaches that have been used and the tentative nature of findings. My concern in this chapter is not to adopt one method or to critique the various kinds of research in progress. Rather it is to point out some implications of the research of cognitive psychology on imagination for the literary study of the New Testament today.

If interpreters are to be faithful to contemporary readers — a task that Pope Paul VI pointed out as their responsibility — they must take into account progress in human self-consciousness that has taken place since the New Testament was written. This self-consciousness experienced a major or "axial" leap in the transition from the medieval world to the establishment of technological culture, that is, between the fourteenth and the seventeenth centuries. During that period "man conceived the idea that he himself might recreate the world of nature to accord with his own imagination" (Richardson: 37). From living in the situation of being within nature and destined to conform to it, human beings started to look on nature as a mechanical system to be manipulated. They came to believe that nature could be "transformed to express the full rationality of man's own mind" (Richardson: 38).

Thus for the first time, the age of human self-consciousness dawned and with it the dream of new behavioral possibilities. Out of that dynamism gradually came an awareness of the unconscious, which paved the way for psychoanalysis with its overwhelming impact on contemporary culture. Freud's work on psychoanalysis, despite the attacks upon it, has been the source of profound insights into the role of the imagination in human experience.

The discovery of the unconscious was in one sense the secularization of what ancient religious thinkers called the ineffable, that is, the unknowable nature of knowledge of God. This new discovery could go two ways. Humans could turn their back on God and adopt what Scripture called a state of "ignorance of God" (Wis 13:1; 1 Peter 2:15), the absence of spiritual discernment. Or humans could grow in awe, overwhelmed by their inability to grasp the divine (Acts 17:23).

Recent studies on the hemispheres of the brain may make it possible to pinpoint and foster imaginative activities in a more scientific way. The study of human self-consciousness is far from over (Singer and Pope). The resulting self-awareness stimulates imaginative activity on many levels. Here it is sufficient to examine briefly three levels: the psychological, the literary and the historical points of view.

1) *Imagination in Experimental Psychology.* After a period of decline because of the predominance of behaviorism, research on the imagination in experimental psychology began to thrive again during the 1960s in areas like image formation, fantasy, dream study and daydreaming. Matthias Neuman gives a brief summary of important findings. These indicate that the imagination was seen to comprise a whole series of imaginal processes and might better

be designated as "imaginal activity" (Neuman: 258).

Anthropological research provided evidence to show that the imagination serves as a force for psychosocial equilibrium, because it acts as "a composing balance between many polarizing forces on various psychic levels to help persons achieve integration, interiorization and intimacy" (Neuman: 262). Many of its "operations function as inherent dynamisms and need not be called into action by conscious decision" (263). Hence, rather than trying to define imagination, Neuman prefers to design a complex system that will contribute to an "integrated theory" by providing "morphological and organic correlation of differing information" (253).

That approach provides a theoretical foundation for the presentation of Kathleen Fischer on the use of imagination in every aspect of Christian life. In dealing with "Imagination and Scripture," she develops three guidelines for interpreting the text: a) attend carefully to the text itself; b) call upon historical and literary criticism; c) celebrate and live the text within the community of faith (Fischer: 34-49). She compares the image of the mythical rainbow that joins heaven and earth as well as the biblical rainbow, sign of the covenant between God and creation after the flood, to the psychological role of the imagination, which "reaches life in its wholeness" (165).

In his attempt to apply psychological data about the growth of self-consciousness in individuals to the development of the imagination, John D. Crossan proposes "very tentatively and theoretically, certain possible stages in imaginative development." Extrapolating from studies in the production and comprehension of metaphors, he proposes "at least four successive steps in imaginative development: the imaginal, literal, metaphorical, and paradoxical" (Crossan: 49-50). After making this suggestion, however, he concentrates upon paradoxical language, especially the parables of Jesus, and links them to "syntactics, pragmatics, and semantics" (61). These — it will be recalled from Chapter 1 — are simply the three networks of every language. They comprise the elements that make language the form of communication proper to the human species, but do not apply the insights of cognitive psychology to an understanding of the imagination. Behavioral sciences gain insights only at a painfully slow pace by means of carefully controlled experiments. It is too early to formulate a theory of the imagination acceptable to all. Some experiments show promise of revealing more about the human psyche by uncovering the role of the rhetoric of persuasion. The mention of rhetoric introduces the second level of the imagination to be looked at here.

2) *Imagination and Literary Criticism.* My focus here is on the New Testament as a canonical text. For Christians it is not a group of private writings containing religious language but that library of religious literature that provides their norms for faith and practice. In this sense the New Testament belongs to "that body of specifically religious writings which religious traditions consider to be foundational, normative, or canonical, of particular moment in establishing the religious tradition" (Cahill: 125). In this context the question surfaces about how writings composed in one stage of human consciousness can still guide those who read the text after there has been a radical or "axial" change in self-consciousness.

The continued popularity of ancient classics, including the New Testament, and their power to strike a responsive chord in contemporary readers illustrate that the axial change in human self-consciousness has not cut off modern readers from an appreciation of these ancient creations. "We live out of the future, understand out of the past" (Hart: 214). By making use of transcultural principles, those who live in a period of deeper self-consciousness are able to understand themselves and their motivation better by reading the New Testament in keeping with improvements in literary criticism. Its techniques facilitate the use of the imagination by helping readers analyze all factors at work in the text. Their resulting synthesis empowers readers to undertake the self-appropriation required "for a genuine encounter with religious traditions" preserved in the New Testament. "An underdeveloped imagination, for example, will find itself shipwrecked in the presence of religious myths that have enriched civilization. An underdeveloped appreciation of language renders the classic religious texts mute" (Cahill: 155).

The prevailing trend in scholastic theology has been to treat biblical texts from a purely conceptual frame of reference rather than to approach them as literary productions. As John Henry Newman complained, this narrow focus often cut religious studies off from the mainstream of contemporary society and decreased the potential healing power they offer to society. Theology's distrust of imagination stands in sharp contrast to western literary traditions. Theologically oriented exegetes have developed methods of interpreting New Testament texts according to their original cultural setting. These historical critical techniques have uncovered what these texts said to their first audience (see Chapter 11). But literary critics see the need of going further. They bring a productive imagination to exegesis in the hope of discovering untapped insights for modern readers by prolonging the text in new forms. This is a theopoetic approach that makes use of images and metaphors drawn from contemporary culture to facilitate a transforming dialogue between the text and today's readers (see Chapter 19).

One evident reason for the decline of the influence of religion in secular society stems from the fact that "imagination is the only means of coping with the mysterious texture of religious meaning and the symbolic universe that each religious tradition creates" (Cahill: 138-139). But instead of unleashing the imaginative power of the New Testament world, the narrow conceptualism of much systematic theology has isolated religion from its healing role in society. By concentrating upon the transcendent features of tradition and technical vocabulary, theology has become captured in past forms and second-level language. Such abstract commentary simply burdens successive generations with the accumulation of past ages.

Since the world of the text is an autonomous world, theological study of it must in some way "enable the reader or hearer to enter the literary universe and to establish step by step a communion with the texts." This assumes "some acquaintance with imaginative symbolism," which I shall consider in the next chapter (Cahill: 122).

On the other hand, "the literary operation can keep the text and its demands at a distance." This allows human imagination freedom to draw out new forms of celebrating the root metaphor of faith (Cahill: 117). To aid this effort is the contribution of literary criticism to a more fruitful exploitation of the history of Christian tradition.

3) *The Imagination in Historical Perspective.* Possibility of finding new ways to exercise the imagination in reading the New Testament is necessarily linked also to the historical development of human self-consciousness, which shapes society by projecting its needs as goals to be attained. By studying earlier forms of its tradition, a society sees possible ways to reinterpret that tradition and to avoid false directions. No effort to achieve fruitful dialog with the New Testament is complete without taking into account the role of imagination in the history of its interpretation. Throughout the Church's history, commentaries on this sacred library mirror contemporary questions that stimulated their publication. Hence, what Ray Hart says about revelation itself provides a basis for a study of the history of that revelation, namely: 1) historical beings are either enhanced or reduced by their imaginative activity; 2) "event-inverbalization language is imaginative language" (Hart: 49).

The creations of New Testament authors were enhanced by the new imaginative synthesis that transmitted the Christ event. For example, as explained in Chapters 6 and 11, the evangelists created the new literary form of "gospel" to communicate the Christ event. Not only were these productions of the sacred writers a revelation but their interpretation in each new generation was an expression of the imaginative process that prolonged the "new way of being human" made possible by the Christ event (Hart: 184). Certainly this way could be misunderstood. Some of Paul's teaching already underwent "subtle deformation" at the hands of Paul's opponents (Patte: 304).

In keeping with the principles of semiotics, the complex character of the imaginative riches of the New Testament is always open to new interpretations that challenge the complacency of the human spirit. The history of its interpretation provides a record of how this conflict of interpretations was waged in all types of situations with varying degrees of success. Many extant commentaries show more concern for the problems faced by their own times than for the original issues that provoked the text. These commentaries serve as a vivid reminder that if its message is to be "good news" in the fullest sense, the gospel must be able to speak its word of healing and reconciliation to every human situation.

In the course of history New Testament interpretation evoked such diverse forms as the homilies of the fathers of the Church, the meditations of the mystics, systematic treatises of the scholastics, countless lives of Jesus, and even the "inscape" of Gerald Manley Hopkins (1844-1889). What response it will evoke in the future remains to be seen. In any given historical moment the power of the tradition manifests itself by the way it illumines the experience of believers and expands their self-understanding (Hart: 273). Religious imagination is not content to repeat the words of the text or past modes of interpreting it. Each age must dialog directly with the symbols of gospel revelation as its way to translate the Christ event for its own needs.

The imagination is the name usually given to the creative human power that undertakes this task of synthesizing tradition anew. But, as explained in the last chapter, the imagination is such a complex notion that philosophers are still not agreed about how to undertake its analysis. Hence, to offer a possible method of bringing the imagination to bear in the interpretation of the New Testament, I will devote the next chapter to some contemporary efforts at reconstructing the thinking process of humans stimulated by the transformation of human self-consciousness. This analysis promises to offer future commentators of the New Testament insights for interpreting its linguistic symbolism.

Sources

Cahill, P. Joseph, 1982, *Mended Speech: The Crisis of Religious Studies and Theology.* NY: Crossroads.

Crossan, John D., 1981, "Stages in Imagination," in Charles E. Winquist, ed., *The Archeology of Imagination. Journal of the American Academy of Religion. Thematic Studies* 48/2: 49-62.

Fischer, Kathleen R., 1983, *The Inner Rainbow: The Imagination in Christian Life.* Ramsey, NJ: Paulist Press.

Hart, Ray L., 1968, *Unfinished Man and the Imagination: Toward an Ontology and a Rhetoric of Revelation.* NY: Herder and Herder.

Neuman, Matthias, 1978, "Towards an Integrated Theory of Imagination," *International Philosophical Quarterly* 18:251-275.

Patte, Daniel, 1983, *Paul's Faith and the Power of the Gospel.* Phila.: Fortress.

Richardson, Herbert W., 1981, *Nun, Witch, Playmate: The Americanization of Sex.* NY: Edwin Mellon Press.

Ricoeur, Paul, 1978, "The Metaphorical Process as Cognition, Imagination and Feeling," *Critical Inquiry* 5: 143-159.

Singer, Jerome L., and Pope, Kenneth S., eds.,1978,*The Power of Human Imagination: New Methods in Psychotherapy.* NY: Plenum Press.

Chapter 17

Imagination, Linguistic Symbolism and Interpretation

The axial changes in human self-consciousness brought about by speculation on the imagination stimulated by the Romantic movement produced what Wallace Stevens called an "enlargement of life" (Stevens: viii). Contemporary "interest in the imagination and its work" is "a vital self-assertion in a world in which nothing but the self remains, if it remains" (171). Stevens describes how human self-consciousness reacts in an age of disbelief: "The world without us would be desolate except for the world within us" (169).

That world within us is still a mystery for, "as yet we have not the faintest idea of the code the brain uses to conceive thoughts, to reason, to speculate, to envision, to symbolize, to visualize, to imagine, to form judgments, to arrive at conclusions, to understand, to be empathetic" (Brown: 306). After years of research on the mystery of that world within us and the historical self-consciousness it engenders, Robert Neville concludes that a decisive factor in forming contemporary civilization has been the death of God philosophy of Nietzsche. It was a "dismissal of reason as the foundation of thinking and culture" (Neville: 10).

Neville's response to this uncertainty is a major project to reconstruct human thinking on the axiological thesis that "thinking is founded on valuation" rather than on reason (12). Eventually he hopes to fill out what he conceives as the four basic structures of thinking, namely, "imagination, interpretation, theory and responsibility" (17). He judges the imagination as basic because it deals with "the dimensions of experience having to do with elementary synthesis," a condition that serves as the necessary background to focus any mental attention. "All thinking...presupposes imaginative synthesis as its experential context" because "imagination gives form to experience," and so there is no thinking without the synthesis it provides (17-19).

Scholastic philosophy constantly warned against the danger of an uncontrolled imagination, but Neville sees religion as dealing with "being responsible in imagination," which is the part of thinking that operates according to the reality of beauty" (Neville: 29-30). In his view interpretation deals with truth; theory with unity, and responsibility with goodness. His four basic structures are present to some extent in all thinking, but imagination links them to images through its role as mediator against alienation on all levels of apprehension, imagery and concept. It does this according to the norm of beauty.

Neville explains the origin of mind, of appreciative feeling and of will as being gathered together in the synthetic imagination (Neville: 118-119, 139-148). In one sense imagination is "entirely private." Yet its synthesis undergirds "the world essential to the social reality of thinking" because a person's private subjective world must be the image of a public world (167-169).

In his development of religion and imagination, Neville illustrates how the synthesizing role of imagination applies to biblical revelation when he examines the link between the mythopoetic creation narratives of Genesis to the biblical account of the origin of evil (Neville: 167-175). Imagination also plays a necessary part on the level of perception by synthesizing the two poles of feeling and intention as expressed in human judgment. The dual role of imagination on that level is: 1) to schematize by integrating new elements into a person's perception of the world, and 2) to particularize one's subjective world "by virtue of conformation, with embodiment and energy" (177-186).

The distinctive quality of imagination on all levels of thinking is its spontaneity. Neville sees the role of imagination as important in all thinking because he considers thinking as basically axiological. This means that thinking is founded in valuation and cannot be separated from total human responsibility. This radical reconstruction of thinking has revolutionary implications for understanding religion and explaining revelation. Neville's theory is also the first thorough phenomenological explanation that gives imagination a place in insuring personal continuity. He is still in the process of developing this reconstruction. As yet he has not spelled out all the implications for religious language in particular, but he underlines the importance of feelings as the matter of experience.

Neville insists on the necessity of attributing sufficient attention to fundamental religious imagery, which devotes much attention to the dimension of space, physical and metaphorical. His observations promise to be significant for those who take biblical language and symbols seriously. A recognition of the interaction between the imagination and religion is crucial in today's secular world because only religious imagery "forms the experience which makes interpretation possible" (Neville: 219-265).

These careful philosophical analyses of Neville are in harmony with Amos Wilder's urgings to cultivate respect for the imagery and symbolism of the New Testament. To apply this reconstruction of thinking to normative Christian writings, modern interpreters will have to deal with their distinctive form of religious imagery in a creative way. In that process they will be able to illustrate how its content maintains its creative power to shape Christian experience (Neville: 284-291).

The next step will be for commentators to integrate this imaginative approach to New Testament symbolism with the linguistic principles summarized in the first part of this study. As explained there, language is a complete system of verbal signs or lexemes, which are conventional symbols. Precisely because language is the mode of communication proper to their species, human beings are called symbolizing animals: "action on the human level is symbolic action." In fact, "man's primordial act as a contemplative being, is the act of symbolization" (Wheelwright:18-19).

In examining the way human language operates, Philip Wheelwright divided language in general and symbols in particular into two types: steno-language (namely, stereotyped or "block" or rigid language) and what he calls depth or tensive or expressive language or symbolism (namely, living, fluid, metaphoric) (20). He sees metaphor as the start of symbol, which can remain living and at least potentially creative perpetually, although it can also become brittle and stale (92-110). He notes how difficult it is to define symbol because, "a symbol points beyond itself, means more than it is." As a human construct, a symbol is a complex reality, consisting of three dimensions: 1) a "referend," what it intends in the concrete; 2) a "reference" or way of conceiving the referend; 3) a "process" of referring (19). In its actual operation metaphorical and symbolic language displays a tension between the concrete "vehicle," that is, its visible, surface form of organization, and its abstract "tenor" or the referential thrust it communicates (Wheelwright: 103).

As a symbolic system language must link present and past with future. Language is the chief means of maintaining the dynamic identity of the group that uses it; it links a people's growth with its tradition and challenges its members to fruitful dialog with their history. By adopting the religious language of the New Testament, believers commit themselves to embark on the symbolic journey of the disciples of Jesus (Mark 1:17-20).

This community of language as a symbolic system generates a new world and a new way of life. The efficacy of symbolic action illustrates the insight of Charles Peirce that, to determine the meaning of any sign, we have "simply to determine what habits it produces" (Morris: v). This test reflects his pragmatic approach. "Significant symbols" are those that permit individuals to play specific roles in society and to grow in deeper self-consciousness. In keeping with such criteria, semiotics plays an important role in affirming the power of religious language in shaping its users, for "culture is largely a sign configuration" (Morris: 207). The link between imagination and semiotics will be explained in Chapter 21.

While faithful Christians have exhibited different styles of living over the great variety of eras, localities and cultures through which they have passed, they remain bound together by the structure of the symbols which they have used to celebrate the common religious origin in the Christ event. As Lynn Ross-Bryant expresses it, through symbol "a door is opened and meaning is revealed to us" (Ross-Bryant: 51). She examines the characteristics of those who have investigated the human experience of the sacred, what is often called religious experience. This experience obviously has close links to the linguistic method of interpreting the New Testament, the "theolinguistics" described in Chapter 13.

Her summary of the findings of that research shows four forms of influence: 1) religious experience involves an immediate awareness of the transcendent, a dimension going beyond ordinary human limits to encounter the totally Other; 2) it results in a transformation of the persons involved in it, and their whole being is touched by it; 3) this total involvement is accompanied by spiritual intensity, the "life of the Spirit" in participants; 4) religious experience changes the world view of these persons so that they see reality in new perspective, from a new horizon. Thus, religious experience is the antithesis of ordinary or secular life, which is experienced as contingent, relative, transitory and fostering personal autonomy (Ross-Bryant: 10-17).

One feature that will mark greater attention to imagination and symbolism in New Testament interpretation will be a greater use of world literature, especially of its imaginative narratives. These may shed light on the narrative form of parables, employed by Jesus when he described the Kingdom of God. The nature of story is to create a "world of

responsibility. Our imagination responds to these creations" (Ross-Bryant: 87).

Although all languages are symbolic and use sign systems, the Judeo-Christian tradition fostered the cultivation
of a system of pregnant symbols that invite New Testament
readers to believe and participate in the divine plan of God
explained in Chapter 13. The role of imagination in the
process of unfolding this plan through normative Scripture
will be discussed in Chapter 22. God's plan centers around
the mystery of the Incarnation, which not only promises
salvation of the whole person, body and soul, but also
"reveals the possibility of this occurring through the life,
death and resurrection of Jesus Christ" (Ross-Bryant: 56).

In a sense all Christian tradition is an ongoing celebration
of this central mystery that keeps breaking the tradition
open in new forms of interpretation, expression and experience. Because the language of religious symbolism is by
nature polyvalent (see Chapter 13), it conveys the sense of
mystery as inexhaustible truth, always capable of revealing
the saving work of Jesus Christ in new ways to meet new
situations. It is always open to new forms of symbolic
expression — what Amos Wilder calls theopoetic (see
Chapter 19).

Tzvelan Todorov, who investigated at great length the
links between symbolism and interpretation, warns that it is
impossible to avoid confusion in any effort to synthesize the
contributions of literary criticism to the interpretation of
religious classics. The terminology is too diverse and fluc-
tuating (Todorov, 1978: 110). At the same time, critics agree
that many interpretations of any classical text are possible.
In fact, to understand a classic is to affirm its complexity,
including a hierarchy of meanings and a variety of resonan-
ces. Hence, the reader must both assimilate this complexity
and adapt it to new situations, that is, respect both its
meaning and its significance for contemporary readers (21-
25).

Todorov himself undertook a review of the history of
New Testament interpretation from a literary point of view.
He calls special attention to the finalistic interpretation of

the Patristic period, that is, the view that Jewish Scriptures point to fulfilment in the New Testament writings (Todorov, 1978: 90-113). He explains also how in the modern period (the period that saw the development of teaching on the imagination) a new system of biblical interpretation prevailed, one based on the philosophy of "liberty and equality for all" (125-164).

The basis of his investigation was his understanding of linguistic symbolism as "that excess of meaning by which the signified overflows the signifier" (Todorov 1974:111, "The symbolized is merely a focalized form of the implicit," and so it needs to be interpreted (127-128). Applying this understanding to the symbolism of Christian allegorical interpretation, Todorov deals with the question of whether this form of interpretation differs from the allegory found in interpreting ancient pagan classics like Homer. His study includes an investigation of the uniquely Christian method of the "four senses" of Scripture used by the Fathers and the medieval scholastics. These are the literal and the three spiritual senses: the allegorical, the tropical or moral, and the anagogic or eschatological (Todorov, 1974: 130-133).

He concludes that biblical symbolism is unique. It belongs to "proportional symbolism," in contrast to the "lexical symbolism" of pagan interpretations. By this term Todorov means that Christian symbolism incorporates typology or the unfolding of the divine plan in history. Christian interpreters presented historical facts in the schema of a "relational of fulfillment" with a gradation of the two sets of events, one preparing for the other and meaningful only in terms of that fulfilment. The first set of events is understood as announcing the second — a dimension unknown to pagan commentators (Todorov, 1974: 133). These conclusions point to the unique role that Jesus played in the formation of the New Testament. The place of imagination in the role Jesus played will be the subject of the next chapter.

It is appropriate to conclude this chapter on imagination and interpretation by calling attention to recent writings of Paul Ricoeur on metaphor. Drawing on "Kant's concept of productive imagination *as schematizing a synthetic opera-tion,*" he attempts "to complete a semantic theory of metaphor with a proper consideration of the role of imagination" (Ricoeur: 149-154). He assigns three steps to this role:

1) seeing, that is, the "function of schematization of the new predicative congruence." This is Ricoeur's terminology for explaining how imagination reveals a kinship between "heterogeneous ideas."

2) picturing or acting as a "pictorial envelope" for the activity of the human mind.

3) fulfilling the "moment of negativity" in the metaphorical process. To achieve "a more radical way of looking at things" imagination suspends the ordinary reference and thus projects "new possibilities of redescribing the world." Ricoeur admits that all of this probing is linked to "a theory of imagination and of feeling which is still in infancy" (158).

Thus Ricoeur brings us back to the same paradox expressed at the beginning of this chapter. He also concludes that increasing importance must be assigned to the imagination in the process of human understanding while recognizing the primitive state of research on the subject.

An important note needs to be added about such research, namely, that it will have to take place in the conscious domain of human understanding. Writing as a product of man as an artist "is controlled by forces which, though part of himself and specifically part of his mind," are forces that are voluntary and conscious (Collingwood: 126). Although these are not the only forces at work in humans, they are what identifies humans as responsible.

Sources

Brown, Barbara B., 1974, *New Mind, New Body. Bio-Feedback: New Directions for the Mind*. NY: Harper and Row.

Collingwood, R. G., 1938, *The Principles of Art*. Oxford: Clarendon Press.

Morris, Charles, 1946, *Signs, Language and Behavior*. NY: Prentice-Hall.

Neville, Robert C., 1981, *Reconstruction of Thinking*. Albany: State of NY Press.

Ricoeur, Paul, 1978, "The Metaphorical Process as Cognition, Imagination, and Feeling," *Critical Inquiry* 5: 143-159.

Ross-Bryant, Lynn, 1981, *Imagination and the Life of the Spirit*. Chico, CA: Scholars Press.

Stevens, Wallace, 1951, *The Necessary Angel: Essays on Reality and Imagination*. NY: Alfred A. Knopf.

Todorov, Tzvelan, 1974, "On Linguistic Symbolism," *New Literary History* 6:111-134.

_____1978, *Symbolism and Interpretation*. Paris: Seuil.

Wheelwright, Philip, 1967, *Metaphor and Reality*. Bloomington: Indiana U. Press.

Chapter 18

Imagination and the Mind of Jesus

Once human beings accept the reality of revelation, they admit the possibility of being able to recognize God's wisdom and will in history. As the last chapter explained, the New Testament pictures that divine wisdom as God's plan for saving his people in Jesus. "The Christian faith and life find their center in the gospel of the revelation of God in the life, death and resurrection of Christ" (Wilder, 1952: 42). This revelation is rooted in the imagination of Jesus insofar as it revolutionized the images of Israel's tradition.

Because Jesus acted as both the climax and the key revealer of that universal divine plan of salvation, Christians have always considered it necessary for them to maintain contact with the historical Jesus who preached the coming of the Kingdom of God. Christian faith "rests on unrepeatable and decisive historical events and its formulation includes an essential intellectual content. But dogma is always mythopoetic and not discursive" (Wilder, 1952: 42). One of the meanings of the Greek term *mythos* is plot, as in a drama. Jesus played out a unique role as the central actor in the divine drama that inaugurated God's Kingdom.

One of the paradoxes of that divine drama is that Jesus left no writings to communicate his mind. He gathered followers and preached the arrival of the Kingdom, but never wrote out for them a written code of belief and practice. Until modern times this never caused problems among Christians because they accepted the New Testament as the normative record of revelation. But modern historical criticism has posed a challenge to the tradition that the words of Jesus found in the Gospels relate his earthly self-consciousness. The name most frequently connected with attacks on the historicity of the Gospels is Rudolf Bultmann. As early as 1926 he wrote, "We can know almost nothing of the life and personality of Jesus." This caused him no difficulty personally because he considered the question of the historical Jesus as "irrelevant" for faith (Marlé: 44).

Bultmann was a leader in developing the methods of New Testament historical criticism that are explained in Chapter 11. But he considered that existential interpretation alone met the faith needs and answered questions that troubled modern believers. His solution was that New Testament language is mythical and foreign to modern modes of thinking; it has to be demythologized or reinterpreted. Development in transcultural sociolinguistics, psychology and the social sciences have made the individualistic and one-sided approach of Bultmann's existentialism a less attractive interpretative tool. As a result, New Testament theology is now in a transitional stage. "The ground is being laid for a new theology of the New Testament, one which is likely to be more satisfactory than any which have appeared to date" (Harrington: 211).

The consciousness of the earthly Jesus, fired by apocalyptic and mythopoetic imagination, no longer seems to be beyond the scope of human scholarship to reconstruct. True, a wide variety of opinions exists on the reliability of the material in the Gospels concerning the earthly Jesus. The disagreement stems from the fact that modern commentators are two literary steps removed from the earthly Jesus, who is available to them only as mirrored in the canonical Gospels. These writings, in turn, are one step removed from the earthly Jesus; they were shaped by the early Church's faith in the death, resurrection and glorification of Jesus.

The trust that the evangelists put in the oral traditions and in the written sources available indicates the sense of identity they felt with the person and mission of Jesus. He came to give his life "as a ransom for many" (Mark 10:45). More than that, recent research in the Aramaic dialect spoken by those living at the time of Jesus points to features from it surviving in the recorded sayings of Jesus.

In contrast to the skepticism of Bultmann and many other form critics, Barnabas Lindars is now convinced that it is possible to reach an understanding of "Jesus' reference to his ministry and to his passion" by the use of the phrase "Son of Man" as preserved in the Gospels. By relying on the Aramaic linguistic evidence, he concludes that the authentic Son of Man sayings are "characterized by irony and reticence on the part of Jesus in speaking about himself, but they also reveal deeply held convictions concerning his vocation from God" (Lindars: viii). This is not the place for a detailed report on these analyses, but they call attention to the need of a more careful study of the language of Jesus. He spoke in a style that was meant to touch as well as teach. He was a master of irony and paradox, as studies on his parables illustrate.

A scholar who has focused attention on the language of Jesus for over 40 years is Amos Wilder, himself a poet as well as a New Testament specialist. While appreciative of the pastoral concern of Bultmann, Wilder recognizes that even in a modern age the human spirit reaches out beyond the borders of the exact sciences. "An age like ours, nourished too exclusively on a rational fare, may legitimately deepen its grasp of existence by the symbolic imaginative vehicles offered by myth, provided that they are constantly animated by and criticized by what is central in the faith" (Wilder, 1950: 119). What moderns need to enter into the mind of the earthly Jesus is not to reject myth but a "constant interpretation and re-interpretation" of "his mythopoetic language that is the vehicle of his saving message" (120).

Wilder's study of the language of Jesus as preserved in the

Gospels indicates that it "had a parallelistic rhetorical character closely related to the forms of Hebrew poetry," and hence it belonged to "poetry in the formal sense." In other words, many of the sayings attributed to Jesus in the Synoptic Gospels point to him as a "charismatic" who spoke in "that kind of heightened and visionary immediacy which inevitably took rhythmic expression" (Wilder, 1952: 7). This is one more indication that "the Church's historical memory of Jesus is inseparable from its faith and message" (Wilder, 1950: 127).

What does the speech of Jesus reveal about his person? A strong "eschatological consciousness," evident in the form and the "secular ethos of his sayings," and in the way he transformed all the "cultural-models" that he employed (Wilder, 1982: 132). Jesus' own sense of fulfilling the law and the prophets permeates the authoritative portrait that Matthew paints of him (Matt 5:17). This sense of the proper moment, the divine *kairos,* gives Christian faith a unique historical depth. The Gospels are documents *"which themselves claim that the veracity of history is integral to the meaning of their message,"* a message that is linked "to certain historical events and a certain historical person" (Robinson: 43).

In terms of providing some understanding of the imagination of Jesus, his parables invite more sustained and elaborate investigation. They represent a complex development in the oral tradition before they were embedded in the individual Synoptic Gospels, from which they receive additional significance. As Wilder says, they contain "successive layers of the great cultural symbols" that Jesus drew upon in formulating his message (Wilder, 1982: 111). It is true that the faith perspective of the early Church could always skew the original thrust of the words of Jesus. Yet indications of the continuing fidelity to the form of his message — even when early preachers shifted away from forms Jesus used — gives confidence that the New Testament witnesses preserved the creative thrust of his message.

The insight of the beatitudes of Jesus, the force with which he either deepened or reversed the direction of the

Mosaic commandments, the striking examples of wisdom in his aphorisms that jolted human complacency — all of these are expressions of a unique spiritual life and creative imagination in Jesus. He brought Israel's image of being God's covenant partner to a new level of intimacy (see Chapter 13).

A similar awareness of tradition as regards the teaching of Jesus is evident in the writings of Paul as apostle to the nations. He distinguishes what he attributes to a command of the Lord Jesus from his own directives (1 Cor 7:10). Thus he was conscious that what he handed on to a new generation was the new imaginative vision that he had received as gift from the risen Lord (1 Cor 11:23). Most probably, this gift came to Paul through the Christian community as the Body of the risen Lord on earth.

A similar responsibility to enter into the vision of Jesus rests upon the Church today. How can New Testament commentators carry out their duty of fidelity to contemporary believers and searchers for truth that Pope Paul VI saw as a necessary complement to fidelity to Christ? The next chapter will look at Amos Wilder's approach through a contemporary theopoetic. It embraces the cultivation of a Christian imagination to insure an avenue of approach to the Spirit of the living Lord Jesus. The "modern temper," as he puts it, needs "the revolutionary substitution of a quite new vehicle and language, responsive to the time, though without surrender of the perennial elements of the Christian revelation" (Wilder, 1952: 144).

Sources

Harrington, Wilfrid J., 1973, *The Path of Biblical Theology*. Dublin: Gill and Macmillan.

Lindars, Barnabas, 1983, *Jesus Son of Man: A Fresh Examination of the Son of Man Sayings in the Gospels in Light of Recent Research*. London: SPCK.

Marlé, Renē, 1967, *Introduction to Hermeneutics*. NY: Herder and Herder.

Robinson, John A. T., 1979, *Truth is Two-Eyed*. Phila.: Westminster Press.

Wilder, Amos N., 1950, "Mythology and the New Testament," *Journal of Biblical Literature* 69: 113-127.

_____1952, *Modern Poetry and the Christian Tradition: A Study in the Relation of Christianity to Culture*. NY: Charles Scribner's Sons.

_____1982, *Jesus' Parables and the War of Myths*. Phila.: Fortress.

Chapter 19

Theopoetic: Amos N. Wilder's Vision of a Renewed Christian Language

Amos N. Wilder began to use the words "theopoetic" and "theopoesis" in print in the year 1972, borrowing them from Stanley R. Hopper (Wilder: 1976: iv). They build on and complement the thrust of the term he previously used, "mythopoetic," which deals with all that can be attributed to a divine cause or influence, that is, to revelation in the strict sense. But theopoetic adds a new element, "a deep impulse in human nature to orient itself in the unknown by pictorial representations, by imaginative dramatizations and narratives" (74). In appropriating the imagery of salvation history as a cosmic drama, the divine plan becomes its *mythos*, its larger plot or world story, and the Christ event is its climax. The images of divine intervention that grew up in the social imagination of the Judeo-Christian tradition all belong to the "prior mythical horizon of the kingdom of God" as Jesus announced it (77-80).

This theopoetic language continues to control the structure of Christian faith and theology and to guide the Church's worship and life. Wilder sees this imagery as now going through a crisis in this secular and post-Christian age. As a critical realist, he recognizes the impossibility of this long tradition of theology and symbolism ever becoming an integral part of the culture again — even for members who remain loyal to the Church. Yet he does not give up on the power of Christian experience to spark our human lives and "transform our outlook" (Wilder, 1976: 76). In this trust he writes as "a traditionalist as one first of all concerned for the renewal of the biblical tradition in our time" (102).

Wilder is convinced that Christians need to accord "a greater role to the imagination in all aspects of the religious life" if they hope to enrich this secular world both as individuals and as a faith community (Wilder, 1976: 2). "Imagination is a necessary component of all profound knowing and celebration; all remembering, realizing, and anticipating; all faith, hope, and love" (2). How to trigger this imagination, and how to sustain its transforming power is the question that Wilder has been addressing with ever greater urgency in recent years by his work on "theopoesis" or religious imagination. This sophisticated outreach will not operate automatically or without sustained effort on the part of the Church.

The crucial element in this form of imagination is its ability to relate divine grace and Christian symbols to the signs of the time. Believers will find in a theopoetic a form of concern that reaches out to appropriate contemporary symbols and dreams as vehicles of healing and of peace. They must let contemporary needs and injustices gestate within their minds and hearts and celebrations. Thus, terms like vision, ecstasy, dream, gestate, plastic and spontaneity figure prominently in Wilder's writing. He uses paradox. On the one hand, "Before the message there must be the vision, before the sermon the hymn, before the prose the poem." At the same time, however, "Before oneiric and chthonic mysteries comes the waking life on earth" (1, 104).

A theopoetic does not try to impose any static program or ideology or hidden agenda. On the contrary, it is flexible and creative. It looks to contemporary culture to provide the starting point for the renewal of the Christ presence of unselfish service in society. Christian imagination is able to make contacts with prevailing symbols to baptize what is redeemable in them. "It is at the level of imagination that any full engagement of life takes place" (Wilder, 1976: 2). The human race will never again live within the sphere of the sacred as the framework of its cultural and social life. In a secular society the role of the New Testament commentator is much more demanding than the office of paraphrasing texts or defining traditional terms or repeating hallowed phrases.

As explained above in Chapters 3 and 4, the elements of every communication event or speech act go far beyond the conceptual matter that is being shared, and that is especially true in religious communication, which is highly emotive. All the speech elements and functions pointed out by Roman Jakobson have to be integrated and synthesized by the imagination, which plays an active role on all levels of thinking — as was explained in Chapter 17. Thus it is impossible to project beforehand the most effective methods for translating the various literary genres that form the New Testament into today's mindset.

Given this situation, the exercise of a theopoetic will not be easy. This form of creative imagination faces a variety of "resistances" from the status quo because it departs from prevailing categories and reigning norms and so threatens human complacency. Wilder sees some of these resistances as rooted in "romantic ideas" of imagination as "something separably aesthetic and irresponsible" and so not in touch with human needs. But he judges that these objects fly in the face of the revelation found in Scripture and tradition, which has always been marked with celebration and spontaneity and has remained open to "symbolic and metaphorical" forms (Wilder, 1976: 41-42). Symbols and images provide the cutting edge for making revelation come alive in every age. Christian symbols face a special challenge among those numbed by overexposure to contemporary mass media. "After all the Bible is a panorama of visions and revelations" (49).

The Society of Biblical Literature recognized Wilder's

influence on biblical research in this century by commissioning a book on him in its Biblical Scholarship in North America series. It is a study by John D. Crossan called *A Fragile Craft*. Readers who wish to locate Wilder's theopoetic in the context of his long career as writer, theologian and church leader will find a critical appraisal there. For this short review of Wilder's concern with imagination, a more specific frame of reference is his long study detailing the close involvement of Christians in artistic movements of their time, *Modern Poetry and the Christian Imagination*. He describes this work as a "diagnosis of our time in terms of its imaginative literature," provoked by the "cultural crisis still in its acute phase" (Wilder, 1952: 257).

If anything, this phase has become more acute. So, working out of his wide range of personal interests, Wilder no longer confines himself to literature. In his *Theopoetic* he appeals more strongly for "the rights of the imagination" (Wilder, 1976: 2). He proposes it as the vehicle to actualize revelation now, because in these apocalyptic times, "it is only at the level of a theopoetic that these contemporary issues can be rightly explained" (5). But what does this elusive theopoetic promise? It will synthesize the resources both of human culture — especially the fruits of the language explosion — and of the Judeo-Christian revelation with its creative theology of the Word. The combination of these two resources could mobilize total human consciousness for the healing of the human race and the world in which it lives.

For New Testament commentators, theopoesis is a call to be open and willing to learn "to read the biblical texts with the tools and approaches employed by our colleagues specialized in literary studies" and to observe what is happening in the arts and in communication (Wilder, 1976: 5). Over and above this personal effort of moral and spiritual discipline and updated techniques, a theopoetic illustrates that, "Any fresh renewal of language or rebirth of images arises from within and beyond our control," namely, in "the idiom of the Spirit" and in the arena of "primordial language and dynamic symbols" — not to mention the realm of the unconscious that plays an ever greater role in human affairs (6). Wilder encourages interpreters to widen their horizons and dialog with domains of reality that a purely rational and discursive critique does not bring into focus.

A creative theopoetic operates on two fronts, corresponding to the two fidelities demanded of biblical commentators by Pope Paul VI in speaking to members of the Italian Biblical Association at their meeting in Rome in 1970. The first is fidelity to revelation, to the biblical text itself and the tradition it generates within the Christian community. The second is fidelity to our age and to all those living in it (Paul VI: 1970). I shall use these two fidelities as guides in summarizing Wilder's suggestions insofar as they provide direction in areas needed to communicate the good news of the Kingdom of God today.

What does fidelity to the New Testament text mean in a modern age? It can be expressed in the traditional ideal of glory, of the "blessedness of the cross" (*hilarotēs*), an experience that "will prompt new tongues, new names, new songs" in a way that satisfies a universal "thirst for liberation." This was the gift of the Spirit that animated early Christian communities (Wilder, 1976: 9-11). God revealed his glory so that creatures could relish, celebrate and share it with one another. Believers dwell in this glory as in their home not only during their earthly pilgrimage but even more fully in the heavenly communion of saints. Hence, a theopoetic's "greatest single contribution," arising from the New Testament revelation, "could be to repossess the mystery of the cross in its glory in a way that would speak to all" (12). Interpreters need to be citizens of their own age, but they also have to know how to "correlate" new findings with "our older traditions" (21).

Ironically, those outside the Christian community at times show profound appreciation for these insights. Here, like John Henry Newman, Wilder sees great danger in a parochial narrowing of the Christian heritage that turns searchers away and provokes them to rebuke church-going believers for their own timid "impoverishment." This lack of openness to "total human experience" keeps believers from

providing the new synthesis of life-giving faith able to nourish this age (Wilder, 1976: 22-23).

The second fidelity called for by Pope Paul VI — namely,
to contemporary individuals and society — searches for
creative means to engage "new cultural situations." Culture
here embraces the new shift in self-consciousness called
forth by the knowledge explosion, feminism, space stations,
threat of nuclear war, water pollution, soil erosion, third-
world poverty, terrorism. All these conditions have created
"a shift in our sense of reality" (Wilder, 1976: 13-16). Instead
of withdrawing from such situations with their problems
and challenges, New Testament interpreters must delve
deeper into the images and anxieties they have generated
among people today and seek bridges by which Christian
revelation will speak to a space age. Drawing upon how the
apostle Paul adapted to new situations, Wilder understates
the interpreter's task: "This requires visionary capacity, at
least as potent as that of the prevailing secular dreams and
idolatries" (26).

A theopoetic will nourish the self-confidence that Christians need to recognize they are not abandoning their faith
when they plunge into the pain of today's world. New
Testament commentators cannot exclude any particular
class of people from their concern. The good news is for
everyone, in every walk of life, in every part of the world.
Only after grasping the whole social situation will they be
capable of addressing its message to people who are caught
in "a dissolution of older patterns."

In our scientific world sometimes the need of imagination
is illustrated by comparing it to the creativity of the artist in
contrast to that of the scientist. Scientists are said to exercise
creative imagination by transcending prevailing limits to
formulate new theories. In so doing they overturn existing
paradigms and produce a radical systems change. Artistic
imagination, on the other hand, is pictured as a creative
exploration of existing reality. It "involves exploiting and
extending the possibilities potential in an existing set of
principles in order to make a presentational pattern." A
"presentational pattern" is "a specific set of relationships

designed to be directly understood and experienced by culturally competent audiences" (Meyer: 179).

Wilder's theopoetic, however, transcends this dichotomy. it strives for a higher order of synthesis, a transcending ecstasy which is "a by-product of a new insight achieved through struggle, whether of the scientist, the artist or the saint." Theopoetic judges all these forms of striving by both the illumination of the Holy Spirit and the depth of Judeo-Christian experience in order "to recognize common features in the creativity of scientist, artist, and mystic" (Wilder, 1976: 60-63).

This effort by Wilder to renew the language of the Gospel draws attention to contemporary studies on the inspiration of the Bible, which will be discussed in the next chapter. For ultimately, "the important thing," says Wilder, is "the revelation" (72).

Sources

Crossan, John D., 1982, *A Fragile Craft: The Work of Amos Niven Wilder*. Chico, CA: Scholars Press.

Meyer, Leonard B., 1980, "Exploiting Limits: Creation, Archetypes, and Style Change," *Daedalus* 109: 177-205.

Paul VI, Pope, 1970, "Exegesis and Hermeneutics," *Osservatore Romano* (October 8, English Edition) 1-3.

Wilder, Amos N., 1952, *Modern Poetry and the Christian Imagination: A Study of the Relation of Christianity to Culture*. NY: Charles Scribner's Sons.

_____1976, *Theopoetic: Theology and the Religious Imagination*. Phila: Fortress Press.

Chapter 20

Inspiration — A Conceptual Dilemma

When used with respect to the Bible, the term "inspiration" is actually an abbreviated way of designating a concept formed by a Greek compound word — first found in 2 Timothy 3:16 — "divinely inspired" or "breathed upon by God." This remark evidently refers to all Jewish Scripture and affirms it as enjoying special power and authority. The probable meaning of this new compound is this passive force, although some few commentators prefer the active sense of "breathing forth God." The word was a new coinage, but not the idea, for the Jews at the time of Jesus considered all their sacred texts as the word of God.

"Though inspiration is mentioned explicitly in only one or two places, the fact that it was mentioned at all was sufficient reason for its purport to be spread over the entire range of the Bible" (Barr: 3). James Barr here alludes to 2 Peter 1:20-21, which speaks of the prophets as being borne up by the Spirit, who gave their words a special authority, for that text affirms God's Spirit as the origin of· all prophecy (Achtemeier: 108). We could also include in these "one or two places" the words of Jesus in John 10:35. He affirms the infallible validity of Scripture, which cannot be "untied," a Greek term usually translated as "annulled" or "destroyed." The Bible itself has no technical language to elucidate the process of inspiration, a term that is prominent today in Evangelical circles. In fact, it contributed to the split in the Missouri Synod of Lutherans (Achtemeier: 13-17).

In the introduction to his study of the Catholic theories of biblical inspiration, J. T. Burtchaell alerts readers to the complexity of this question: "Biblical inspiration, after all, is not a single problem; it forms the nucleus of a constellation of problems" (Burtchaell: 4). Bruce Vawter calls that study "a well-researched scholarly presentation of its subject" (Vawter: 182). I recommend it to readers who are looking for a detailed review and perceptive critique of how this "constellation of problems" was dealt with in the 150 year period after the Enlightenment, but that topic is beyond the scope of this chapter.

Sufficient for our purpose is to note Burtchaell's conclusion that what happened as regards inspiration in Catholic scholarship has been "an unhappy controversy" (Burtchaell: 280). He attributes the lack of intellectual progress in handling the question to three weaknesses: 1) "an uncritical defense of official authority," 2) "an obsession with inerrancy," and 3) "a crude theology of divine-human collaboration" (281-295).

New interest in the charism of inspiration was stimulated by the revival of Thomism under Pope Leo XIII (1878-1903). The outstanding pioneer in Catholic biblical studies at that time was M.-J. Lagrange, founder of the Dominican school of biblical studies in Jerusalem. He brought together three elements — the Thomistic theory of instrumental causality, a special knowledge of ancient Near Eastern literary forms and a theory of sensible and historical appearances —in an effort to formulate a modern comprehensive theory of inspiration. The death of Leo XIII and the Modernist controversy cut short Lagrange's research on this subject before it reached maturity. Support for him faded quickly as a result of the policies of Pope Pius X. "By 1910, after only three years of papal exertion, it was all over. And as the bickering fell silent, so did practically all creative biblical scholarship" (Burtchaell: 230, a judgment that Vawter quotes with approval on page 124).

Not until 1943 did creative Catholic biblical scholarship again receive papal encouragement with the encyclical of Pope Pius XII, *Divino afflante Spiritu.* It was written under the influence of his Jesuit friend, Augustin Bea, whom he appointed rector of the Pontifical Biblical Institute in Rome. In terms of intellectual climate, this encyclical marks a "thaw" that "invites a second spring of biblical studies" (Burtchaell: 239).

Catholic scholars returned to the approach of Lagrange and the scholastic "prophetic model" of inspiration. The prophetic model assumes the immediate activity of God upon the faculties of the sacred writer in the production of the inspired text that God wants to appear. It assumes that each text of the Bible has "*an author*" (Achtemeier: 100). The new freedom allowed by Pope Pius XII in Catholic biblical scholarship produced a flurry of activity, especially in the subject of the social nature of inspiration by such authors as J. L. McKenzie and Karl Rahner before Vatican II (Hoffman: 448), and followed later by Vawter (see below).

In 1947 Pierre Benoit wrote an introduction and commentary for the recently translated tract on prophecy of Thomas Aquinas' *Summa Theologica.* It forms part of the *gratiae gratis datae* or charisms of the Holy Spirit. St. Thomas never wrote a tract on biblical inspiration as such. Benoit's method is essentially that of a scholastic commentary. Burtchaell's evaluation is typical: "Benoit's theory and its painstaking defense is not likely to draw support except from those committed to a 13th century system of psychology" (Burtchaell: 244).

Burtchaell himself struck an optimistic note when he foresaw "a new heyday of creative speculation on biblical inspiration." But this creative outburst failed to materialize, at least within the fifteen years following his historical survey. The increasing sophistication in biblical studies that encouraged his optimism and which he recognized as the

necessary basis for a more fruitful approach to basic problems is not yet evident in recent speculation on inspiration
among Catholic biblical scholars (276-277).

One long study on biblical inspiration did follow soon
after Burtchaell's book. It was a treatise by Bruce Vawter
that dealt with three areas: the concept of inspiration, its
biblical terminology and its history. Vawter illustrates the
need of a sense of history to appreciate how Christians have
read the New Testament since Patristic times because the
Bible is "for the most part a 'secular' literature," that is, a
"loose collection of casual works of disparate kinds" (Vawter: 1-2, 20-42). The way the Bible grew and was continually
reinterpreted points to an attitude different from modern
orthodoxy by "men of the Bible," even those whose writings
appear in it. "Within the Bible itself religion was not a
scriptural religion in the sense that it later, and especially
after the Reformation, became normal to suppose" (Barr:
4).

Bruce Vawter devotes the major part of his study of
biblical inspiration to a historical review of the question and
a critique of the various forms of approach. He points out
the lack of any real progress in coming to an understanding
of the term in the Middle Ages. "Christian thinking has
succeeded only in reacting in one way or another to the
scholastic synthesis, it has never succeeded in replacing it."
Not that all accepted the scholastic approach through the
analogy of instrumental causality. In fact, a large segment of
biblical scholars "has simply abandoned it as no longer
revelant" (Vawter: 44).

Vawter himself finds the scholastic approach "far too
intellectual a notion, far too much bound up with the propositional concept of revelation inherited from the Fathers"
(Vawter: 57). He also rejects the *sensus plenior* or "fuller
sense," at least in its crude form that would give Scripture a
meaning "fuller than that intended by the inspired writer,
precisely because he is the instrument of a principal author,"
namely, God. "However, it is very possible that a more
sophisticated concept of *sensus plenior* may be defended by
an appeal to linguistic analysis," that is, when human lan-

guage itself "has been made the instrument of divine communication" (115).

At the end of his detailed monograph Vawter limits his synthetic thrust to offering five suggestions "regarding a desirable theology of inspiration" (Vawter: 157). He concludes that in every case inspiration "was something," so that Scripture is more than "human words only," because there is some "kind of divine intent in the working of the Bible" (167). Following the proponents of inspiration as a social charism, Vawter shifts the locus of inspiration from individuals to the community: "inspiration is to be thought of as primarily a community charism." Not that it doesn't influence individuals, but it does so in an analogous way, according to their role in bringing about books that are different from one another (162-164). He also insists upon "its permanent and dynamic character," in that inspiration was "not only the spiritual influence responsible for the Bible's origins but also that which sustains it as a medium of speech" (170).

The focus of this dynamism is thus upon the word of God as an abiding power within the believing community through which the Holy Spirit's saving wisdom is available to every generation. This emphasis on the empowered word provides a link to the more literary approach to inspiration. Among Catholic scholars, the literary approach was championed by Luis Alonso-Schökel, who did his research on inspiration before Vatican II.

He too disclaims any intention of writing a "treatise" or "strictly scientific study" of inspiration. Rather, he will expose the topic "in terms that are imaginative and synthetic" (Alonso-Schökel: 14). He is caught between the sense of divine revelation as a personal communication given by "way of imagination" and "its fundamentally intellectual character" (29).

As a theologian with a literary background, he shows how the fathers of the Church and scholastic theologians have used analogies to describe the divine "condescension" of God in cooperating in a unique way with humans to produce the inspired writings (Alonso-Schökel: 49-50). To the list of traditional analogies for inspiration — God as the author of Scripture, dictation, the human writer as (muscial) instrument or tool or messenger — Alonso-Schökel introduces the image of human authors as literary characters created by the skill of the divine author of the Bible story. He depends upon this plastic image to take the edge off the mechanistic ring of instrumental causality. "Our idea of inspiration must be spacious enough to allow room for all its concrete expression and all the varieties of the inspired books" (91). But he remains within the scholastic tradition of viewing the charism as a *gratia gratis data*, "gift freely given" by the Holy Spirit for building up the Church.

What Alonso-Schökel brings to his writing on inspiration is a keen sensitivity to language. He complains that the treatises on inspiration produced by "the neo-scholastic movement" show "complete ignorance of the depth of the problem of language." Yet he offers only "a complement to the traditional approach." He follows the principle that, since inspiration pertains to language, a deeper understanding of language will prepare commentators "to penetrate into the mystery of inspiration" (Alonso-Schökel: 121-124). In fact, before going into an explanation of the psychology of inspiration, he devotes two chapters to explaining functions and kinds of language (134-173). It is not that the activity of the Holy Spirit can be scrutinized by psychology, but that "human literary activity" can be.

Alonso-Schökel is sensitive to the criticism that his approach is artificial in that "biblical authors are not romantic or modern poets," and that their relationship to their community was much different from that of a modern self-conscious and creative artist (Alonso-Schökel: 180, 223). So he also examines the sociology of inspiration "from the angle of language and literature" (225). The end result of his research is a series of probes that reveal how complex the question of inspiration is. He writes without dealing explicitly with "reader response criticism," discussed above in Chapter 7, but touches on many of the same concerns. A text reaches its perfection "*quando lector fit auctor*" (when the reader becomes author: 275) or when a passage is represented in the liturgy or public recitation to be celebrated by the whole community (296-305).

Rather than taking the narrow view of inerrancy as propositional truth, Alonso-Schökel prefers to talk about five kinds of truth found in the Bible: 1) truth as the self-revelation of God in the mystery of Christ; 2) truth according to literary modes, or knowledge by familiarity; 3) truth as witness enjoying "an existential quality, capable of engaging the whole man;" 4) truth as dialogue, and 5) logical truth (Alonso-Schökel: 309-324).

Paul Achtemeier sums up the current state of the question on inspiration in his study. A sharp division now exists among biblical scholars about how to deal with inspiration and the related question of the authority of the Bible. On the intellectual right, conservative Evangelicals take a rigid stance in affirming "the Bible's inspiration and inerrancy" in the strongest terms. They have come together for two international meetings to formulate positions on biblical inspiration and inerrancy. "The evangelicals will, for example, not tolerate any approach that casts into doubt the historical authenticity of events reported in the Bible"(Scear: 157). To the left, the so-called liberal view holds that the Bible is simply "the human record of the Judeo-Christian tradition." "All can be understood within the normal perimeters of human activity" (Achtemeier: 43, 48).

Those within the mainstream of Christian faith, who want "the Bible to continue to play a meaningful role in their lives" seem to be at a loss about how to compose a tract on inspiration that will speak to the modern believer. Thus Achtemeier calls his study "only a preliminary sketch" (17, 19). He concludes by asserting that a valid understanding of inspiration is the result of "the interaction of three key concepts," namely, "the tradition of the faithful community, the situation facing that community, the compiler of those traditions into a piece of literature" (Achtemeier: 123). His stress is on process, both in the formation of Scripture and in the import that it has through the Spirit's continued guidance of the community of believers (161).

In contrast to broadening the concept of inspiration,

Thomas Hoffman has recently proposed a more narrow definition of the charism. He laments that by "syndoche" the term inspiration has come to embrace the whole area of normativeness, canonicity and inspiration of the Bible (Hoffman: 451). Instead of trying to encompass the long and complicated process by which the Bible as a whole, and the New Testament in particular, were formed, he prefers "a phenomenological analysis of the 'terminal sense' of inspiration, the inspired books themselves" (454). Advantages that he finds in this approach include leaving room for the continued operation of the Holy Spirit in the text as well as admitting that other writings could be inspired without being canonical Scripture and, therefore, normative for the Church.

But even Hoffman's approach is analytical and conceptual and does not provide a model to incorporate the special role of imagination to describe the process of divine-human cooperation in producing the books of the Bible. The following chapter will investigate that approach.

Sources

Achtemeier, Paul J., 1980, *The Inspiration of Scripture Problems and Proposals.* Phila.: Westminster Press.

Alonso-Schökel, Luis, 1965, *The Inspired Word: Scripture in the Light of Language and Literature.* NY: Herder and Herder.

Barr, James, 1983, *Holy Scripture: Canon, Authority, Criticism.* Phila.: Westminster Press.

Burtchaell, James Tunstead, 1969, *Catholic Theories of Biblical Inspiration Since 1810: A Review and Critique.* Cambridge: Cambridge U. Press.

Hoffman, Thomas A., 1982, "Inspiration, Normativeness, Canonicity, and the Unique Sacred Character of the Bible," *Catholic Biblical Quarterly* 44: 447-469.

Scear, David P., 1983, "International Council on Biblical Inerrancy: Summit II," *Concordia Theological Quarterly* 147: 153-158.

Vawter, Bruce, 1972, *Biblical Inspiration*. Phila.: Westminster Press.

Chapter 21

Inspiration and the Imagination

What stance is to be taken in the face of the failure of Catholic scholars to arrive at an acceptable description of the nature of the divine inspiration of Scripture, a failure outlined in the last chapter? Some commentators simply ignore the question. That is an unacceptable solution because every commentator operates out of some methodological presuppositions. As Sandra Schneiders warns, "To be unaware of these presuppositions does not make them inoperative, it simply makes them ideologically tyrannical" (Schneiders: 52). An appreciation of that special form of divine influence called inspiration is important for all those participating "in the work of interpreting the text as the Church's normative source of revelation," for their goal is to help the New Testament "become word of God in the community of believers" (57).

A modern understanding and appreciation of inspiration — whether it is called a charism or not — must be that of today's post critical age, namely, it must incorporate the growth of self-consciousness fostered by the Enlightenment. For this reason Schneiders insists upon the need for a "nonreductive hermeneutical theory" that will enable interpreters to respect "the philosophical and the literary dimensions" of the New Testament (Schneiders: 58). She recognizes that such a theory does not yet exist, but lists three elements it must include: 1) a philosophy of language to treat the text as an independent, abiding "linguistic entity," 2) a theory of knowledge that allows for validation of method, and 3) an ontological basis for understanding the "truth claims that the meaning of the text makes upon one" (58-63; compare Eco: 5).

I wish to move a step beyond the theoretical basis into the area of method and suggest how attention to the language explosion fits in with "the crucial importance of the role of the Holy Spirit" in the production of the New Testament. For "the Spirit works *through* the normal processes of human understanding, and neither independently of them nor contrary to them" (Thiselton: 90). But the form of understanding proper to human communication is linked to language. In fact, outlining the history of New Testament interpretation, Thiselton speaks of the beginning of the eighteenth century as "the third period when the study of language as such was seen as the necessary hermeneutical tool" for understanding the text (116). In this chapter I want to follow that lead by taking into account the insights about language described in Part I and integrating them into an understanding of inspiration.

For this purpose the use of semiotics holds out the most promising hope of producing a theory of inspiration that respects the way literary works are created. "The concrete literary work is a sign constituted by the correspondence of the signifier with the signified." It is the creative unity of form and matter that "constitute a unitary whole" (Alonso-Schökel: 7). A semiotic approach built soundly upon language as a system of verbal signs is subject to all the constraints of any sign system. Because it goes beyond purely linguistic rules, semiotics bridges a gap that—as Thiselton is at pains to point out — must be addressed by interpreters: "Whereas linguistics (or semantics) concerns only the horizons of the text, hermeneutics concerns both those of the text and those of the interpreter" (Thiselton: 120).

Semiotics incorporates into textual studies a "logic of culture" and fits texts into the wider network of human communication by means of signs. Surely Huberto Eco is correct when he says that it is still too early to write a treatise on semiotics (Eco: 7-8). So he entitles his foundational study *A Theory of Semiotics.* In it he develops both a theory of codes—"the conditions under which the message may be communicated" (15) — and a theory of signs, for there can be no sign except in a cultural context. He defines signs first as "*everything,* that on the grounds of a previously established social convention, can be taken as *something standing for something else*" (16). Later he adopts a more technical definition: "a sign is always an element of an *expression plane* conventionally related to one (or several) elements on a *content plane*" (48).

Working from this technical definition Eco concludes, "Properly speaking there are not signs but only *sign-functions*" (49; he also uses the expression "sign-vehicles," as on p. 57). By this expression he means two things: 1) a sign is not a "physical entity," that is, a thing with an enduring fixed identity existing in nature, and 2) a sign is not a "fixed semiotic entity," but is rather the coming together of elements "from two different systems of two different planes and meeting on the basis of a coded correlation" (Eco: 49; compare Eugene Nida's comments on signs in Chapters 4 and 10). The meaning function a sign embraces is such that "as Peirce said, a sign can be explained only through another sign" and so on without limit (61). This principle establishes a necessary link between semiotics and society. "The semiotic object of a semantics is the *content,* not the referent, and the content has to be defined as a *cultural unit* (or a cluster or a system of interconnected cultural units)" (62).

In such a cultural framework Peirce's theory of interpretant is crucial for understanding how a sign works for two reasons: 1) it "guarantees the validity of the sign, even in the absence of the interpreter," and 2) it "brings a process of *unlimited* semiosis" (Eco: 68). This semiotic approach both grounds a scientific exegesis and demands continual linguistic interpretation of texts in new situations. It provides a basis for affirming the authority of inspired canonical texts and explains why the Church must be concerned about preserving these texts in accurate form and about watching over their interpretation and their translation into new languages and cultures (see Chapter 11). The semiotic principle at stake — "New messages can restructure the codes" — flows from the very creativity of language (161). Semiotics thus offers the qualities needed to meet Wilder's concern that contemporary theopoetic become a vehicle for biblical revelation.

At the same time, my chief concern in this chapter lies at the other end of the literary process, namely, how to link the activity of the Holy Spirit known as inspiration to the origin of the New Testament writings. From a purely critical point of view, advances in semiotics "removes many phenomena from the realm of individual 'creativity' and 'inspiration' and restores them to that of social convention" (Eco: 269). A recognition of the cultural nature of sign provides both a challenge and an opening to deal with the activity of the Holy Spirit in and on the writers of this liturgical library. The inspired authors are part of a culture; they use the same language codes available to other members of their society. As communicators they were also concerned "with extra-semiotic circumstances," which they wished to evaluate and critique and so either support or reinforce or change the codes prevailing in their society according to their new understanding of God's will (Eco: 158).

The individual New Testament authors had the responsibility of synthesizing some aspect of the Christ event and of translating the new cultural conditions it created into text for use by the emerging Christian community. Recent Catholic theories of inspiration — even those that stress its social nature — have not linked the question of divine influence to semiotics, "the process by which empirical subjects communicate, communication processes being made possible by the organization of signification systems" (Eco: 316). Yet biblical writers interacted with their community and with the surrounding society. They learned as well as taught by words and ideas as signs.

Here Robert Neville's ongoing project of a reconstruction of thinking, explained in Chapter 17, provides a new factor that promises to shed light on the role of inspiration. His rigorous philosophical approach to imagination as a form of thinking contrasts with the vagueness of Wheelwright, who builds upon Coleridge but expands his insights along the lines of literary criticism. Coleridge attributed a creative function to secondary or productive imagination, as outlined in Chapter 15. He coined the term "esemplastic" for this role from the Greek phrase that means "to shape into one," because active or productive imagination fuses and synthesizes images (Wheelwright: 372).

From his hypotheses Wheelwright discusses four areas in which the imagination functions. For these areas he creates the four designations: confrontative, stylistic, archetypal and metaphoric imagination (Wheelwright: 78). He adopts this procedure in keeping with his goal of distinguishing expressive or depth language from literal or steno-language. But his method neither clarifies the nature of imagination as such nor does it offer help for understanding how God cooperated in a special way in producing the New Testament.

Where then does imagination fit into human personality in general, and in particular how does it relate to human intelligence? Some writers portray imagination as a faculty distinct from the intellect, and so as a form of human activity distinct from thinking. If so, the imagination would have to be located in the unconscious, because the three methods of human animation — sensing, feeling, thinking — do not admit of a fourth method. This is why scholastic philosophers locate the imagination among the internal senses and see it as necessarily dealing with individual objects. For them, if the imaginative faculty fell outside the area of human intelligence, it would have to be located in the unconscious and as such would be outside of the range of rational observation (Joy: 45-48).

In contrast to the scholastic approach and the vagueness of Wheelwright, Neville's solution has many advantages (see Chapter 17). He sees imagination as a form of thinking, but one distinct from the human analytic method of reasoning. In his view the intelligence has two functions: 1) to analyze by the use of reason, and 2) to synthesize or intuit, by the use of the imagination. Imagination then is not confined to dealing with concrete objects, but performs a role of synthesizing on all levels of understanding.

At every stage of thinking the imagination enables human beings to incorporate all available data into an integrated vision. It takes its model from the openness of visual experience, which grasps a whole panorama simultaneously, in contrast to verbal thinking, which involves progression. Imagination is "the means by which contradictory elements can be entertained at many levels" (Joy: 49). As a faculty, the imagination verifies the maxim that a picture is worth a thousand words. A single image integrates a great amount of information into an integrated vision in contrast to the method of words in breaking apart and analyzing specific concepts.

But the imagination has the further power of drawing out the relevant qualities from all the levels of knowledge available and then synthesizing them so as to provide insight to the thinking subject. A modern image that helps envision this role of the imagination is the electronic scanner. It oscillates between frequencies to pick out significant objects. The imagination's power to hold multiple elements and levels of reality in creative tension enables humans to compare, select and synthesize their religious experiences. It helps them develop affective responses to God's saving interventions as narrated in the New Testament, which reflects upon and communicates the mysteries of faith and offers them as a subject of contemplation and encouragement.

In such a context Charles Kraft, as an anthropologist-linguist-theologian takes up the question of "how the Holy Spirit goes about leading culture-bound human beings 'into all truth' (Jn. 16:13)." He answers: "via the human perception of those to whom he speaks. Since the channel is culture-bound human perception, the receptors do not understand supracultural truth absolutely" (Kraft: 129). He is primarily concerned with hearing the Bible today, but also applies the principle in the production of each biblical writing — the subject I am concerned with in this chapter. "In the original revelation of biblical materials God also worked in terms of culturally conditioned human perception." This includes the psychological situation and needs of hearers (130). Kraft goes on to illustrate how "anthropological and communication models...yield exciting perspectives on revelation and inspiration" (169).

To explain the "divine-human participation," Kraft proposes the "interaction-participation model," with God leading and guiding and the human author participating (Kraft: 203). "God worked *with* them and in terms of their normal cultural, psychological and intellectual limitations rather than against them" (204). He sees the divine-human interaction process as dynamic but never attempts to explain how it functions. He quotes with approval the work of Bruce Vawter on inspiration, discussed in the previous chapter. Kraft's chief preoccupation is to uphold the human dimensions of inspiration in response to a "closed conservatism" that equates inspiration with inerrancy and denies any human element in the Bible as God's word (203-213).

Is it possible to specify that human dimension of inspiration more explicitly by taking into account findings of research in the social sciences? Recent work by experimental psychologists on the imagination as a human function enables us to plot the direction of human cooperation with God's Holy Spirit. This research also supports Neville's view of human thinking as axiological. "Imagination is viewed as the central kernel of consciousness and an important means of access to the individual's world." It can serve as an investigative tool to enable a person "to differentiate, to experiment with, and to integrate fantasy and reality" (Shorr: 97). Here is an area where divine-human cooperation might be investigated to show how inspiration is linked to the role of Scripture in the healing of human ills. New Testament interpreters will have to be open to newer types of research — like waking dream theory or Jung's active imagination or biofeedback — because at present no standard definition or universal understanding of the imagination exists.

One type of imagination deserves consideration before looking at actual examples of imagination in the New Testament in the next chapter. That is what Sandra Schneiders has labeled "paschal, or Christian, imagination" (Schneiders: 65). This type forms an appropriate transition because it refers to "the new self-understanding and possibilities of existence that became available to the first generation of Christians after the resurrection of Jesus" (65). This is the experience that Paul describes in a variety of ways: as being "baptized into Christ" (Rom 6:3), as "putting on Christ" (Gal 3:27), that is, as being clothed in Christ, or simply — to quote Paul's favorite phrase — as being "in Christ" (Gal 3:28 and over 100 times in his letters).

The experience that Schneiders describes embraces "the whole cognitive-affective capacity" of the believer in a synthetic "wholeness" that is the feature of the imagination (Schneiders: 65). She reasons, "I suspect that the emergence and exercise of the paschal imagination in the production of the text as witness comes close to what we mean by the concept of inspiration, that the paschal character of that imagination is what gives the entire text its Easter quality" (65). Such inspiration is apparently what "makes the text a locus of revelation." The text then exists to be "actualized in contemplation." The New Testament then begins to be read with the answering imagination of faith that is "the transformation of the interpreter" (66).

Sources

Alonso-Schökel, Luis, 1975, "Hermeneutical Problems of a Literary Study of the Bible," *Congress Volume Edinburgh 1974; Vetus Testamentum Supplement* 28: 1-15.

Eco, Umberto, 1979, *A Theory of Semiotics*. Bloomington: Indiana U. Press.

Joy, Morny, 1983, "Explorations in the Philosophy of Imagination: The Work of Gilbert Durand and Paul Ricoeur," in J. V. Apczynski, ed., *Foundations of Religious Liberty*. College Theology Society: 1982 Annual Publication: 45-53.

Kraft, Charles H., 1979, *Christianity in Culture: A Study in Dynamic Biblical Theologizing in Cross-Cultural Perspective*. Maryknoll, NY: Orbis Books.

Schneiders, Sandra M., 1982, "The Paschal Imagination: Objectivity and Subjectivity in New Testament Interpretation," *Theological Studies* 43: 52-68.

Shorr, Joseph E., 1978, "Clinical Use of Categories of Therapeutic Imagery," in Jerome L. Singer and Kenneth S. Pope, eds., *The Power of Human Imagination: New Methods in Psychotherapy*. NY: Plenum Press.

Sloan, Douglas, 1983, *Insight-Imagination: The Emancipation of Thought and the Modern World*. Westport, CT: Greenwood Press

Thiselton, Anthony C., 1980, *The Two Horizons: New Testament Hermeneutics and Philosophical Description with Special Reference to Heidegger, Bultmann, Gadamer and Wittgenstein*. Grand Rapids: Eerdmans.

Wheelwright, Philip, 1959, *The Burning Fountain: A Study in the Language of Symbolism*. Bloomington: Indiana U. Press.

Chapter 22

The Role of the Imagination in Forming the New Testament

As the liturgical library to guide the Christian Church, the New Testament is a collection of 27 short occasional writings in four different literary genres. They were composed during the period that followed the early oral preaching of the good news of God's salvation in Jesus Christ for believers who had not seen him on earth. Christians of later generations needed further understanding of their faith as well as encouragement to prepare for the return of the Lord Jesus in glory. They needed instruction on how to build each other up in Christ-like love and thus preserve a counter community in the world of paganism threatening to engulf them.

This framework of faith, love and hope sets the boundaries of both the New Testament community and of its canon or collection of normative Scripture. All of these writings are linked to the Christ event by religious imagination in that they embody a new form of creative synthesis. They all evoke a response of mind, heart and lifestyle to the intervention of God in Jesus.

Amos Wilder often calls attention to the "abundant and

significant" role that vision plays in the New Testament writings. It is linked to the "eschatological consciousness" that shaped the early Christian Church with its "sense of world-transformation in course and ultimate goals within reach" (Wilder: 71). At the same time this dynamic imagination was rooted in great cultural symbols and "the most ancient epiphanies" of Israel. The Church maintained this identity as it survived various cultural changes (77-79). What the Christ event inaugurated was "a liberation of human speech and a new grasp on reality" that "ignited a war of myths," which flared into conflict between official Judaism and the Christian vision of what Israel should be. "This war of myths is dramatically orchestrated in the Book of Revelation with a full repertory of ancient cosmological motifs" (81-83).

Wilder relies upon this cosmic-eschatological imagination to see the focal image that Jesus used, namely, "the Kingdom of God," as rooted in "the oldest covenant imagery, especially the covenant of creation." So Jesus identified his opposition "with Satan and the demons" (Wilder: 85). And Paul followed along the same imagery by affirming that anyone in Christ Jesus is "a new creation" (2 Cor 5:17).

In this chapter I offer some examples of the imaginative activity of the inspired writers of the New Testament to help readers become more familiar with the role that the emotive dimension of these writings plays in stimulating the Church to carry on the saving mission of Jesus. I am not attempting any kind of complete commentary but simply give significant examples of literary imagination from each of its four literary genres. These are meant to encourage a more active reader response to other New Testament texts and thus lead to the desired goal that the "reader become author."

1. THE GOSPELS

An important study of the Gospel of Mark as an imaginative construct has been produced by the Canadian scholar David Stanley. His aim is to help those who make or direct "the Spiritual Exercises of St. Ignatius Loyola" (Stanley: 5).

Mark took "a *living* tradition, created originally by the earliest disciples of Jesus," and composed a document "which became a vital factor especially at public worship" by which "believers fed their faith and lived out their Christian commitment" (5-6). The most striking imaginative feature of the Gospel of Mark is "the dynamic orientation by St. Mark of his entire Gospel to the Cross" (13). This direction has prompted Mark to structure his narrative from the first to the third predictions of the passion (8:21—10:45) as an invitation to follow Jesus through suffering and obscurity. That is what it means to embrace the path of discipleship on one's journey to the Kingdom of God (18).

What Stanley illustrates throughout his reflections is that Mark's "specially graced reception of the tradition must be sharply distinguished from any process of data-gathering" (Stanley: 19). The result is a "profoundly meaningful introduction to the Christian life of faith" that never ceases to amaze and draw its readers powerfully into the circle of discipleship (18).

Stanley's study is a model of how a careful attention to the text can recognize and stir up the religious imagination. He points out that today's Christians do not have to suspend their imagination in reading the New Testament. On the contrary, they will profit by learning "to appreciate the values for a deepening involvement with Jesus offered us by the sacred writer's imagination" (95). In reality, Mark's method of presenting his Gospel points back "to the use of imagination in the evangelical tradition" (106).

A different method of using the imagination appears in the Gospel of John, who does not produce a great number of scenes, as do the writers of the Synoptic Gospels. John's is rather a contemplative imagination, one that prefers to draw out the theological and spiritual richness of a few incidents by inviting readers into a dialog with the mystery the incident reveals. For John, the life and death of Jesus is a revelation of the life-giving truth that makes believers free. He illustrates this by dividing the ministry of Jesus into a series of literary "signs," each consisting of two parts, namely, an action of Jesus plus an interpretative discourse.

John uses the same method for the passion, except that he inserts the interpretative discourse first in the form of the long interchange between Jesus and his disciples at the Last Supper. Then follows the action of Jesus in the form of the whole passion narrative. Because the passion-glorification of Jesus is the great sign, John spends five chapters explaining its significance in the complex discourse material of 13:31—17:26.

One imaginative technique that he uses within this discourse material (as well as elsewhere in his Gospel) is the "revelation pattern" (see Chapter 6). On the surface the interchange between Jesus and his disciples looks like an ordinary dialog, but a more careful analysis shows that much of it is built upon a special pattern of interchange that involves three elements. These elements are: a) a revelation by Jesus; b) a question or objection by interlocutors, who speak out of a confused or superficial stance; c) a clarification by Jesus of his original revelation (Reese, 1972: 321-322).

When read in the light of the death-glorification of Jesus, these revelation patterns, which are six in number in this part of John's Gospel, spell out the deeper meaning of how Jesus' laying down of his life effects our salvation. It results in the sending of the Holy Spirit and makes possible for believers to look forward in hope to follow the glorified Jesus into the dwellings of his Father. Rather than a scandal or stumbling block to believers, the return of Jesus to the Father through "an obedient act of self-giving" is the very life of the community, but it still "calls for interpretation." This revelation pattern is the imaginative technique by which John invites his readers to "know" the Christ event, that is, to experience its saving power (Reese: 322).

To give an example of John's imaginative style in composing this section, I will comment on one of these revelation patterns, the one that contains the famous description of Jesus as way, truth and life (John 14:1-6):

a) The revelation (John 14:1-4). Jesus encourages his disciples to persevere in faith in him and in the Father because the Father has many "dwelling places," which

Jesus is now going to prepare for them. He alludes to the truth that Jesus dwells in the Father and the Father in him. His departure by a self-sacrificing death is going to open up dwelling places in the Father. They have only to follow in the same way, namely, by a life of service, to enjoy companionship with God forever.

b) Objection (John 14:5). Doubting Thomas acts as the interlocutor. He is on the superficial level. He thinks that Jesus is speaking about some journey through physical space and wants to know the destination.

c) Clarification by Jesus (John 14:6). Jesus explains that his revelation deals with spiritual transformation by responding in the famous maxim that has prompted so many comments in the course of the exegesis of the Gospel of John: "I am the way and the truth and the life." What is crucial for understanding this saying is to recognize that it is a clarification by Jesus. It cannot be understood apart from the context and imagery of the revelation pattern. The principal image is that of the road or "way," and the other two words are added solely to clarify this image in relation to the glorification of Jesus as the true life-giving Exodus to the Father. Jesus is the fulness of revelation in that he communicates God's saving presence to believers. Jesus is the way that is "true" in the sense that he is reliable and unerring for the salvation of believers.

This key image of "way" is reinforced by negative statements in the second half of Jesus' clarification. Only "through me," Jesus insists, can they have access to the Father (De la Potterie: 915-916). This repetition is in keeping with the nature of Hebrew verse style (called parallelism), which repeats in different words or images the first half of the verse. This style may well provide evidence for the tradition that Jesus spoke as a poet, as Wilder suggests (see further in Chapter 23). This poetic style is in keeping with John's method of presenting the discourses of Jesus. Readers are invited to commit themselves to Jesus by imitating his total orientation to the will of the Father. This passage synthesizes the role of Jesus as celebrated in the opening hymn of John's Gospel (933). Hence, this short revelation pattern provides a good example of the need of readers to pay careful attention to both form and content in John's Gospel in order to nourish their belief, which is the objective he proposed in writing as he did (John 20:31).

2. APOSTOLIC LETTER

The Letter of James is sometimes presented as a series of moral exhortations loosely held together like a string of pearls. Yet more careful attention to its vocabulary, images, repetitions and balanced structure reveals that it is a highly imaginative way to communicate a "profoundly eschatological attitude" (Reese, 1982: 82). To share his core message of the law of freedom, James locates it like a precious jewel in the center of a rich setting. The setting takes the form of a double circle of wisdom material, the inner circle being the warnings or threats of chapters 2 and 4, and the outer circle being the exhortations of chapters 1 and 5. "All the exhortations and threats are directed to the heart of the letter" (83). The frequent use of paradox "mirrors Christian life as this community experienced it" (83).

Use of the homily form in the inner circle to warn members of the community provides James with the occasion to employ strong language and striking images. He wants to make sure that his readers do not relegate eschatology to the next world. So he urges them to "foster a living faith," for it alone will show them "the superiority of the eschatological kingdom over the 'world'" (Reese, 1982: 85). From start to finish this letter is a striking display of the synthesizing power of the imagination. Christian "teachers" learn how to celebrate that eschatological kingdom by keeping their attention focused on the final judgment (James 3:1). Their wise tongues are the rudders that must guide the Church through the stormy seas of this life to the port of eternal peace.

3. ACTS OF THE APOSTLES

This book is a brilliant synthesis of the shifts that the

Church went through from its origin as the small apostolic band located in Jerusalem to its status as the universal community established in Rome, the center of the inhabited world. The author's creative imagination appears in many ways. For example, he "dramatizes for his readers Peter and Paul and Stephen speaking on certain occasions" as part of their role in proclaiming the Good News (Brown: 61).

But here I want to illustrate briefly how this imagination is displayed in the sermon of Paul spoken to the elders of the community of Ephesus (Acts 20:18-35). That speech is a carefully structured composition that belongs to the literary form of the "farewell discourse." It portrays Paul toward the end of his career as saint and hero of the community offering his last word of advice for believers. Every Christian is called to bear witness to the full plan of God with a readiness to embrace the cross of Jesus. Paul instructs the community overseers and elders in their additional responsibility to nourish the Church of God. He includes warnings against false teachers, wolves who will seek to tear the community apart after he has gone.

The discourse then serves to portray Paul as model of orthodoxy, integrity and missionary zeal. The concluding quotation from Jesus, that it is better to give than to receive — not found in any of the Gospels — provides a striking link between Paul and the Lord Jesus, who still guides his Church through the presence of the Holy Spirit. This scene illustrates the power of the productive imagination of the author of Acts to produce an edifying synthesis of apostolic faith that helps to nourish the Christian community down through the ages.

4. THE BOOK OF REVELATION

This is the only Christian apocalyptic writing accepted as part of the Church's official or canonical New Testament. Without explicitly quoting the Hebrew Bible, it integrates over 500 allusions to it into its picture of the Church's ongoing struggle against the kingdom of Satan on earth.

The author offers this book as a "revelation of Jesus Christ" (Rev 1:1).

More specifically, it is a vision which he sees through "a door opened in heaven" (Rev 4:1). This does not mean that John did not have to use his creative imagination in organizing the text. On the contrary, the opening vision in Chapters 4-5, which serves as the setting for the whole series of revelations, pictures a heavenly liturgy modeled on the Sunday liturgy of the early Church. John uses the gathering of the local bishop, his elders and the laity as model for the heavenly vision. By this brilliant use of imagination John illustrates the truth he will dramatize through the whole writing, namely, that the Church is guided throughout its history by God's wisdom and powerful presence — for God has made his people "a kingdom of priests and they shall reign upon the earth" (Rev 5:10).

In conclusion, these few examples from the New Testament illustrate how the inspired writers of the early Church made striking use of their imaginative powers to compose the works that make up Christian Scripture. Their creativity invites modern commentators to ask what role imagination should play today in the Church's reading of these books. That will be the topic of my final chapter.

Sources

Brown, Raymond E., 1983, "Preaching in The Acts of the Apostles," in John Burke, ed., *A New Look at Preaching*. Wilmington: Michael Glazier, 59-73.

De la Potterie, Ignace, 1966, "Je suis la Voi, la Vérité et la Vie (Jn 14, 6)," *Nouvelle Revue Theologique* 88: 907-942.

Reese, James M., 1972, "Literary Structure of Jn 13:31 — 14:31; 16:5-6, 16-33," *Catholic Biblical Quarterly* 34: 321-331.

_____1982, "The Exegete as Sage: Hearing the Message of James," *Biblical Theology Bulletin* 12:82-85.

Stanley, David M., 1982, *The Call to Discipleship: The Spiritual Exercises with the Gospel of St. Mark.* The Way Supplement 43/44.

Wilder, Amos N., 1970, "Myth and Dream in Christian Scripture," in Joseph Campbell, ed., *Myths, Dreams and Religion.* NY: E. P. Dutton, 68-90.

Chapter 23

Imagination in a Contemporary Reading of the New Testament

I conclude this introductory study of a linguistic method for interpreting the New Testament by recalling once more the twofold task that Pope Paul VI assigned to biblical interpreters. They must be faithful not only to the text but also to modern readers of the Bible. The first part of this study presented modern methods of analyzing and understanding how language works, following especially methods developed by Eugene Nida and Roman Jakobson. Since the New Testament books (like every other writing) are a series of communication events, their readers must know how language communicates in order to feel the full impact of their message. Part II has investigated the role that creative imagination has played in both the formation and the understanding of these writings.

Now I call attention to some of the most promising methods recently proposed for incorporating the imagination into this ongoing process of interpreting the New Testament. More and more, from Coleridge to Robert Neville, the imagination is being identified with the power of synthesizing. As such, it plays a significant role in the interpretative process as it is conceived by Sandra Schneiders. She states that the goal of interpretation is "to appropriate the message of the text in its integrity." In that task she includes "the dialectical illumination of the meaning of the text and the self-understanding of the reader" (Schneiders: 77). Every New Testament text is necessarily polyvalent or pluri-significant because it is simultaneously speaking to the tradition and to the needs of new audiences who must integrate its messages into their situation but also their situation into its world. "The work generates various valid interpretations in different readers" (77). Consequently, the entire history of New Testament interpretation has a bearing on understanding its message. This history reveals hidden facets of its richness and contributes to the fusion of horizons between text and readers, bringing them to understanding, appreciation and ultimately to application or conversion.

The perduring value or referent of a religious text is "the religious truth claims of the text about God and humanity." This quality flows from the nature of religious language as symbolic (others prefer the term "metaphorical"), that is, as encompassing both a literal and a "deeper, secondary signification which is attainable only in and through the primary signification" (Schneiders: 79). The organic link between all levels of meaning creates an important role for the imagination, which has power to synthesize these levels of reality. Its task is productive and creative in contrast to a fanciful "eisegesis" or arbitrary reading of meaning into a text.

At this point it should be clear that the inclusion of the role of imagination in the interpretation of the New Testament does not depend upon adopting some particular philosophical method. Imagination does not introduce some extraneous process into interpretation but flows from the very nature of language as a sign system — described in Part I of this book. The particular networks of language — lexemes and the syntax they involve, semantics and pragmatics — operate on both deep and surface levels. Hence, the resulting sign effects demand explanations by further signs according to some kind of interpretant, as C. S. Peirce showed and semiotics elaborates (see Chapter 21). This interpretative process continues indefinitely, generating ever new interpretations in changing contexts, as explained above in Chapter 1.

This is the power of language that Amos Wilder constantly calls attention to in his study of the language of the good news. His reflections on the narrative form illustrate the synthesizing role of imagination. He looks upon the new interest in language as grounding "our new interest in story," which reaches back to "the all but universal form of storying we call 'myth'." Among ancient peoples myths, along with ritual, served an important function for "they held the world together" (Wilder: 354). In the New Testament the Gospels and Acts are part of this long narrative tradition, serving as a vehicle for the Christian imagination. "Mark builds up the setting of Jesus' teaching in parables, thus lending a heightened tenor and acoustics to this vein of his teaching. Jesus challenges the imagination of his hearers with such rubics as 'Listen!' or 'What think you?' or 'With what comparison?'" (356).

Wilder calls attention to the fact that the sayings of Jesus which are preserved in the Gospels betray a lyrical quality. He sees the parable style of Jesus and the lyric poets as "not far apart." Both "usher us into a heightened world or another world" (Wilder: 356). In an approach that agrees with many of the insights of Schneiders, he sees stories as involving and transforming hearers: "they speak to our wrestlings with necessity and fatality." Taking up the imagery of text as texture, Wilder points out that the "weaving of all such fabulation" is like a tapestry "with differing threads, stitches, and pigments" (357).

Readers learn from the imaginative synthesis of New Testament writers — examples of which I gave in the last chapter — to "recognize that daily life is itself mysterious and dynamic." The flexibility of oral narrative was captured in writing so that the "kinds of interests" generated by story continued to operate to fulfill its role of proclaiming the good news. Contemporary commentators are challenged to continue the work of the inspired authors: "the ensuing weaving of storied experience must maintain its sway over the imagination by a combination of surprise (novelty) and familiarity (recognition)" (Wilder: 358). An imaginative commentator will alert readers to the "inchoate fund of longings, anguish, obscurities, dreams" that Jesus explored in his parables and linked to the quest for the Kingdom of God. In a variation of his own principle, quoted in Chapter 1, that, "The language of a people is its fate," Wilder affirms, "Our language worlds are the only worlds we know!" (361).

The religious imagination of the New Testament writers guided them in mobilizing their language competence to record significant speech acts or communication events with the hope of incorporating new believers into the mysterious and therefore inexhaustible language world of Jesus. A gap exists between that world and the modern situation. To dialog with the New Testament, readers today need a bridge over that gap. Translation builds that bridge. This is the specialty of Eugene Nida, whose interest in improving the quality of biblical translation provided much of the direction for Part I of this study. As an anthropologist-linguist, Nida is able to translate in the fullest sense. On the one hand, he brings the world of the religious experience of Jesus and the early Christian community into the grasp of modern readers. On the other hand, he carries these readers over into the New Testament culture.

The world in which Jesus lived was one of primary religious experience and vocabulary. Jesus enjoyed a vivid experience of God and his fatherly presence. Nida lists the chief qualities of primary religious language as: figurative, dramatic, creative, instructional, nontechnical, inconsistent, and not given to explaining itself (Nida: 285). Over the centuries — as Christian theologians used, reused and interpreted the Christ event — this language has been overshadowed by the secondary language of institutional Christianity. Nida characterizes secondary religious language as: repetitive, explanatory, expository, full of technical terms, discursive, demythologizing (285-286). Hence the challenge to today's New Testament commentators: to become competent not only in the mechanics of language as such but also in the way that key Christian terms have shifted meaning because of cultural differences between the world of Jesus and modern society. "Cultural patterns are constantly in a state of change," and, "Languages are constantly changing on all levels, but preeminently so on the level of meaning" (293).

In addition to a knowledge of sociolinguistics, New Testament commentators also need discernment to empathize with the original communication event. This is the challenge of "theopoesis" that strives to update Christian tradition in terms of its appeal to contemporary hopes and needs. With the world bending under unprecedented social and economic burdens, believers strain for strength to undertake their task of applying the good news to healing human ills. In accepting this challenge, they are being faithful to the Christian tradition because throughout history "the prompting to story was pragmatic, a matter of fateful orientation and survival" (Wilder: 363).

It is to the question of world survival that Frederick Herzog addresses himself in dealing with imagination and liberation. He explains how entering into the proper imagination-milieu enables us to hear the message of the good news — the call to engage in "God's battle for justice" (Herzog: 228-229). Why is such a frame of reference or — in linguistic terms — "universe of discourse" necessary? Because without it believers are unable to make the basic decisions for the Kingdom of God. And the heart of New Testament concern is precisely to generate commitment to the ongoing saving plan of the Father of Jesus Christ. The power to be loyal to him comes not from human resources but from the Holy Spirit whom Jesus sent upon his followers. Paraphrasing 2 Corinthians 5:17, Herzog states, "If anyone is in the messiah Jesus, this person is a new creation" (229).

From this analysis of the presuppositions, principles and direction of liberation theology, he warns, "Unless in our situation the Bible functions as the primary 'text' of God's action, all we end up with is our own action" (Herzog: 232). Because the New Testament was written in one culture and must today be interpreted in a different one, its interpretation has to be kept free of the presuppositions of cultural bias. Sociolinguists have developed two techniques to insure that: the emic method, that is, working within the institutions and attitudes of the original culture, and the etic or transcultural method of translating these values into the receptor culture. The aim of both methods is to prevent the text from being co-opted by any set of presuppositions. Use of both methods makes clear the limitations under which every interpreter labors.

Herzog lists some conditions for avoiding misuse of the text: "Obviously, the gospel does not offer us a social program for the twentieth century. But Messiah Jesus does liberate us for justice/love in the contemporary situation" (Herzog: 238). This approach widens the scope of religious language. It is not limited to a purely rational analysis of the biblical text but embraces all connotations of the text as a communication event or speech act with all the factors and functions delineated by Roman Jakobson (see Chapter 3). The text is not heard as religious until it leads to choice in the life of readers.

Liberation as a semiotic approach (that is, treating the text as a series of signs) illustrates that interpretation is an ongoing series of choices. As Charles Peirce taught, a sign is tested by the habits it produces. Human life, like human language, is in constant flux. Humans can never make one ultimate, absolute, unchanging, definitive statement that brings interpretation to a halt. And so the task of New Testament interpretation never ends. Its aim is to apply the gospel message of salvation to every age and situation.

George Montague addressed this ongoing aspect of New Testament interpretation in his 1978 presidential address to the Catholic Biblical Association of America. He recognized the positive elements of the historical critical method described above (see Chapter 11). Yet, his premise was that any method which leaves "many questions unanswered" about what the New Testament is saying to the Church and to the world today cannot be an adequate hermeneutical method (Montague: 2-3). He pointed out a fact that professional commentators often ignore: that all readers are familiar with language. Hence, "The meaning of a text may be more available to the ordinary reader than the historical exegete is willing to admit" (8).

Montague's own experience as a teacher brought home to him some of the shortcomings of the historical critical method. Two of these are: 1) its failure to affirm the role of "the community which the word-event creates," and 2) its failure to recognize that "that community affects the interpretation of the word." His line of argument is that the lived experience of the community of the word enfleshes its promises "in the context of human experience and relationships" (Montague: 9). This living community witness to the revelation displays the power of the text more creatively than abstract philosophical analyses. The resulting display of community responsibility challenges the imagination of readers and especially of those interpreting the text in the context of preaching. The danger for preachers is to become more interested in personal applications than in communicating how the text addresses the believing community.

It is this community dimension that is decisive in Montague's "teaching paradigm," in which he incorporates elements of synthetic imagination that make for a fruitful hearing of the biblical text. He does not propose to offer a "total hermeneutic," but only a "complex and tentative" list of eleven features that should form part of the concerns of those professing to teach a method of understanding Scripture (Montague: 13-16). Most of this teaching paradigm —as is to be expected in the setting of his address — is concerned with rational activity on the part of the interpreter. But Montague also pays tribute to the imagination by including the need to celebrate the text. Celebration, which may take a variety of forms, is a real encounter with the text in a synthetic mode. Ultimately, understanding occurs "in a larger holistic experience in which alone the discovering of meaning can be brought to term" (17). In other words, no human capacity or need can be ignored in the process of interpreting the good news.

Sources

Crystal, David, 1981, "Generating Theological Language," in J.-P. van Noppen, ed., *Theolinguistics*. Brussels: Studiereeks Tijdscrift Vrije Universiteit 8:265-281.

Herzog, Frederick, 1978, "Liberation and Imagination," *Interpretation* 32: 227-241.

Montague, George T., 1979, "Hermeneutics and the Teaching of Scripture," *Catholic Biblical Quarterly* 41: 1-17.

Nida, Eugene A., 1981, "Semantic Reinterpretation of Primary Religious Vocabulary," in J.-P. van Noppen, ed., *Theolinguistics*. Brussels: Studiereeks Tijdscrift Vrije U. 8:283-294.

Schneiders, Sandra, 1981, "The Foot Washing (John 13:1-20): An Experiment in Hermeneutics," *Catholic Biblical Quarterly* 43: 76-92.

Wilder, Amos N., 1983, "Story and Story World," *Interpretation* 37: 353-364.

Conclusion to Part II

These brief indications of how the imagination is being incorporated into current attempts to achieve a better understanding of the New Testament form an appropriate close to this study in two ways: 1) They show some new ways that scholars are taking as representatives of the believing community to make the Church's normative liturgical library more intelligible and accessible to a wider audience. 2) They can also serve as a springboard for concerned students who are looking for direction for starting a personal dialog with the New Testament world. For the key lesson of all hermeneutic is that every end is a beginning. Interpreters stand on the shoulders of those giants who have broken the bread of the good news to Christians throughout the history of the Church. By using both old and new wisdom they can carry the message of the New Testament further. Every interpreter's part in the ongoing quest for gospel truth and value is to offer new students a goal for them to surpass.

The linking in this study of insights from contemporary semiotics to investigations of religious imagination is a step toward an interdisciplinary approach to studying the New Testament by incorporating advances in both language study and the human sciences into progress in theology. This method will enable interested believers to achieve greater communion with their normative Scriptures not only for personal nourishment but also that they may have a part in the Church's effort to offer light and healing to the world.

The linguistic component is necessary to analyze the inspired texts, to break them open for comprehension and guidance. The imaginative component makes possible the new synthesis that looks to contemporary needs. The dynamism generated by the interaction of these two forces stimulates the life of believers individually and as a community. Both are needed in the process by which believers commit themselves entirely to the text and allow the text to carry them into the mystery of God that is Jesus Christ.

New Testament Index

Author-Subject Index